13th International Joint Conference on Natural Language Processing and the 3rd Conference of the Asia-Pacific Chapter of the Association for Computational Linguistics (IJCNLP-AACL 2023)

System Demonstrations

Nusa Dua, Indonesia
1 - 4 November 2023

ISBN: 978-1-7138-9001-0

Printed from e-media with permission by:

Curran Associates, Inc.
57 Morehouse Lane
Red Hook, NY 12571

Some format issues inherent in the e-media version may also appear in this print version.

Printed with permission by Curran Associates, Inc. (2024)

Association for Computational Linguistics
209 N. Eighth Street
Stroudsburg, Pennsylvania 18360

Phone: 1-570-476-8006
Fax: 1-570-476-0860

acl@aclweb.org

Additional copies of this publication are available from:

Curran Associates, Inc.
57 Morehouse Lane
Red Hook, NY 12571 USA
Phone: 845-758-0400
Fax: 845-758-2633
Email: curran@proceedings.com
Web: www.proceedings.com

IJCNLP-AACL 2023

The 13th International Joint Conference on Natural Language Processing and the 3rd Conference of the Asia-Pacific Chapter of the Association for Computational Linguistics

Proceedings of the Conference (System Demonstrations)

November 1 – 4, 2023

The IJCNLP-AACL organizers gratefully acknowledge the support from the following sponsors.

Platinum

Gold

Silver

Order copies of this and other ACL proceedings from:

Association for Computational Linguistics (ACL)
209 N. Eighth Street
Stroudsburg, PA 18360
USA
Tel: +1-570-476-8006
Fax: +1-570-476-0860
acl@aclweb.org

Message from the General Chair

Welcome to IJCNLP-AACL 2023, the 17th International Joint Conference on Natural Language Processsing (IJCNLP) and the 3rd Conference of the Asia-Pacific Chapter of the Association for Computational Linguistics (AACL). The conference will be held in Nusa Dua, Bali, Indonesia, during November 1-4, 2023.

The joint conferences of IJCNLP and AACL are organized by alternating leadership in the Asia-Pacific region, in odd years by Asian Federation of Natural Language Processing (AFNLP) and in even years by AACL, except when the annual meetings of ACL are offered in the region every three years, in which case the conferences will be offered and organized solely by ACL. This year, the conference is organized by AFNLP.

As President of AFNLP, I have formed the Conference Coordination Committee (CCC) last year with executive members of AFNLP: Sadao Kurohashi (Vice President), Min Zhang (Secretary), Liang-Chih Yu (Honorary Treasurer), and Minghui Dong (Web Master). Xuanjing Huang has participated in the meetings of the committee as AACL Representative. I am truly thankful for their dedication in the initial stages as CCC members, in particular during the selection of the Local Chairs together with the conference venue and the nomination and appointment of General Chair and Program Committee Chairs, and, after it is decided that I also serve as General Chair of the conference, for their service as respective chairs throughout the conference preparation stages. Their continued support has been of tremendous help and is much appreciated.

I would also like to thank deeply the entire organizing committee of the conference for their hardwork and superb handling of difficult situations, most of all due to the much limited time to address their respective tasks.

- Program Committe Chairs: Yuki Arase, Baotian Hu and Wei Lu have managed the most critical task of establishing the main program of the conference, which includes, among many others, forming and coordinating the Program Committee, constructing the call for papers with a timely theme track, overseeing the review process on both Softconf and ARR, making decisions on paper acceptance, selecting keynote speakers and putting together the program schedule, and most of all communicating with the reviewers, authors, and other committee members over numerous times during the entire process. This is a formidable task, and their efforts for leading to its successful completion are so much appreciated.

- Tutorial Chairs: Yun-Nung (Vivian) Chen and Sadao Kurohashi have gone through the tutorial proposals to select six tutorials that are well balanced both topically and geographically, actively fostering diversity and inclusion.

- Workshop Chairs: Kehai Chen and Lun-Wei Ku have gone over the workshop proposals to select eight strong workshops, NLPMC, WIESP, Eval4NLP, SocialNLP, SEA, FinNLP, NLInt, and ArtOfSafety.

- Demo Chairs: Sriparna Saha and Herry Sujaini have overseen the process of selecting papers among those submitted to the system demonstration session independently of the main program.

- Publication Chairs: Minghui Dong and Kotaro Funakoshi have put together all the documents and articles to construct the conference proceedings expertly, cordially and in a timely manner.

- Sponsorship Chairs: Min Zhang, Satoshi Sekine, Haofeng Wang, and Zhongqing Wang have worked hard to solicit funding to support the conference, and successfully, despite the short time to operate. We are all much grateful to the funding organizations for their generous help.

- Finance Chair: Liang-Chih Yu has always been the person to consult whenever any financial issues arise. Things are not yet fully over at the time of preparing for this message, but are believed to come to self-sustainment, with some room for financial aid as well, thanks to the valiant efforts of all the people involved.
- Website & App Chair: Juntao Li has worked single-handedly and dependably to reflect all the requests to post important news at our conference homepage.
- Publicity & Social Media Chairs: Koustava Goswami and JinYeong Bak have worked to disseminate information over social media as widely as possible whenever there are notable events for the conference.
- Handbook Chairs: Yasuhide Miura and Yunita Sari have worked very hard to meet the deadline for the conference handbook when there is really not much time left. The help of Sonoko Miura as Conference Handbook Designer is also gratefully acknowledged.
- Faculty Advisors to Student Research Workshop (SRW): Hyeju Jang, Yugo Murawaki, and Derek Fai Wong have worked to oversee the SRW, in particular communicating with its chairs, Dongfang Li, Rahmad Mahendra and Zilu Peter Tang. The efforts of the faculty advisors and SRW chairs are much appreciated.
- Diversity & Inclusion Chair: Hwanhee Lee has worked to resolve requests for financial aid, mostly in the form of registration waiver, and as amicably as possible, under a strict limit on granting such requests.
- Registration Chair: Dessi Puji Lestari has worked to oversee the process of registration, together with the kind help of Minghui Dong as the manager of the registration site.
- Local Chairs: Derry Wijaya, Ayu Purwarianti and Adila Alfa Krisnadhi have worked to resolve practically numerous issues, many times beyond the duties of local chairs, after successfully bidding to host the conference in Nusa Dua, Bali, Indonesia. It is with much gratitude and respect that I commend their efforts to the fullest.

In summary, I can only say that their sense of duty and responsibility has been critical to meeting and resolving so many difficulties that we faced along the way. Many, many thanks to all of them.

The mode of the conference has been determined early on to be hybrid, considering the fact that we are not fully over the coronavirus pandemic. However, it has not been quite clear until very recently whether we would need, and can afford, the top-notch professional service of an on-demand video platform such as Underline for a hybrid conference. I am very grateful to all the chairs for the remarkable patience and very happy with the concerted decision to go for the service of Underline, albeit in a limited scope. I wish to thank kindly Damira Mrsic and Sol Rosenberg, representatives of Underline, for the patience and expert help. I also thank Richard Gerber for the help with our use of Softconf.

The Local Chairs made a proposal to host the conference in Nusa Dua early on, but it took all of us a long time to finally come to a decision to choose Grand Hyatt Bali, Nusa Dua, Bali, Indonesia for its exceptional location in the region as the conference venue. Its daytime temperatures are expected to reach 31°C, with the nighttime temperatures of around 24°C. I wish a very pleasant time for all the off-line participants of the conference and an equally memorable time for all the on-line participants.

Welcome to the conference and Nusa Dua!

IJCNLP-AACL 2023 General Chair
Jong C. Park
Korea Advanced Institute of Science and Technology (KAIST)

Message from the Demo Chairs

We extend our sincere gratitude to all of you for your invaluable contributions and enthusiastic participation in this year's conference. The diversity and excellence of the demonstrations showcased in the proceedings reflect the collaborative spirit and cutting-edge research within the natural language processing community. Your dedication to advancing the field has not only enriched the conference but has also set a high standard for innovation and academic rigor. As Demo Chairs, we are inspired by the quality of work presented and are confident that the insights shared will resonate within the community, fostering continued growth and collaboration. Thank you for making IJCNLP-AACL 2023 a resounding success, and we look forward to witnessing the impact of your research in the broader field of natural language processing.

On a similar note, we extend our heartfelt appreciation to the distinguished individuals who have graciously served as meta-reviewers for this year's conference. Your invaluable guidance, meticulous oversight, and expertise have been instrumental in maintaining the high standards and quality of the submissions. Last but not least, we extend our sincere appreciation to the dedicated individuals who have served as reviewers for this year's conference. Your expertise, careful evaluations, and constructive feedback have been invaluable in ensuring the scholarly rigour and quality of the submissions.

Sriparna Saha, Indian Institute of Technology (Patna)
Herry Sujaini, University of Tanjunpura

Organizing Committee

General Chair
Jong C. Park, Korea Advanced Institute of Science and Technology (KAIST)

Program Committee Chairs
Yuki Arase, Osaka University
Baotian Hu, Harbin Insitute of Technology (Shenzhen)
Wei Lu, Singapore University of Technology and Design

Tutorial Chairs
Yun-Nung (Vivian) Chen, National Taiwan University
Sadao Kurohashi, Kyoto University

Workshop Chairs
Kehai Chen, Harbin Institute of Technology (Shenzhen)
Lun-Wei Ku, Academia Sinica

Demo Chairs
Sriparna Saha, Indian Institute of Technology (Patna)
Herry Sujaini, University of Tanjunpura

Publication Chairs
Minghui Dong, Institute for Infocomm Research, A*Star
Kotaro Funakoshi, Tokyo Institute of Technology

Sponsorship Chairs
Min Zhang, Harbin Institute of Technology (Shenzhen)
Satoshi Sekine, RIKEN, AIP
Haofeng Wang, Tongji University (Shanghai)
Zhongqing Wang, Soochow University

Finance Chair
Liang-Chih Yu, Yuan Ze University

Website & App Chair
Juntao Li, Soochow University

Publicity & Social Media Chairs
Koustava Goswami, Adobe Research India
JinYeong Bak, SungKyunKwan University

Handbook Chairs
Yasuhide Miura, Fujifilm Corporation

Yunita Sari, Universitas Gadjah Mada
(Conference Handbook Designer: Sonoko Miura)

Faculty Advisors to Student Research Workshop
Hyeju Jang, Indiana University-Purdue University Indianapolis
Yugo Murawaki, Kyoto University
Derek Fai Wong, University of Macau

Diversity & Inclusion Chair
Hwanhee Lee, Chung Ang University

Registration Chair
Dessi Puji Lestari, Bandung Institute of Technology

Local Chairs
Derry Wijaya, Monash University Indonesia
Ayu Purwarianti, Bandung Institute of Technology
Adila Alfa Krisnadhi, University of Indonesia

AACL Representative
Xuanjing Huang, Fudan University

Senior Programme Committee

- Tulika Saha, University of Liverpool, United Kingdom
- Deepak Gupta, National Library of Medicine, NIH, United States
- Naveen Saini, Indian Institute of Information Technology Lucknow, India
- Sandeep Mathias, Presidency University, India
- Dipankar Das, Jadavpur University, India
- Sudip Naskar, Jadavpur University, India
- Vivek Kumar Singh, Banaras Hindu University, India
- Manas Gaur, University of Maryland Baltimore County, United States
- Tirthankar Ghosal, Oak Ridge National Laboratory, United States
- Kitsuchart Pasupa, King Mongkut's Institute of Technology Ladkrabang, Thailand
- Rudra Murthy, IBM India Research Limited
- Raj Dabre, NICT, Japan

Programme Committee

- Zishan Ahmad, Indian Institute of Technology Patna, India
- Ramakrishna Appicharla, Indian Institute of Technology Patna, India
- Sujoy Bag, Indian Institute of Technology Kharagpur, India
- Shubham Chatterjee, University of Glasgow
- Subrata Das, Indian Institute Of Technology Patna, India
- Kishalay Das, Indian Institute of Technology Kharagpur, India
- Anindya Sundar Das, Indian Institute of Technology Patna, India
- Baban Gain, Indian Institute of Technology Patna, India
- Soumitra Ghosh, Fondazione Bruno Kessler (FBK), Italy
- Utkarshani Jaimini, Artificial Intelligence Institute, University of South Carolina, United States
- Raghav Jain, AI-ML-NLP Lab, Indian Institute Of Technology Patna, India
- Prince Jha, Indian Institute Of Technology Patna, India
- Ratnesh Joshi, Indian Institute of Technology Patna, India
- Kaveri Kale, Indian Institute of Technology Bombay, India
- Raghvendra Kumar, Indian Institute of Technology, Patna, India
- Sandeep Kumar, Indian Institute of Technology Patna, India
- Gitanjali Kumari, Indian Institute of Technology Patna, India
- Krishanu Maity, Indian Institute of Technology Patna, India
- Santosh Kumar Mishra, Indian Institute of Technology Patna, India
- Prabir Mondal, Indian Institute of Technology Patna, India
- Jose G. Moreno, Paul Sabatier University - IRIT, France
- Rudra Murthy, IBM India Research Limited
- Dipanjyoti Paul, Indian Institute of Technology Patna, India
- Subham Raj, Indian Institute of Technology Patna, India
- Kaushik Roy, AI Institute, UofSC, United States
- Sovan Kumar Sahoo, Indian Institute of Technology Patna, India
- Sukanta Sen, Zoom Video Communications Inc.
- Apoorva Singh, Indian Institute of Technology Patna, India
- Gopendra Vikram Singh, Indian Institute of Technology Patna, India
- Chanchal Suman, Indian Institute of Technology Patna, India
- Deeksha Varshney, Indian Institute of Technology Patna, India

Table of Contents

TRAVID: An End-to-End Video Translation Framework

Prottay Kumar Adhikary
NIT Silchar, Assam, India
prottay71@gmail.com

Sugandhi Bandaru
NIT Silchar, Assam, India
bsugandhi99@gmail.com

Subhojit Ghimire
NIT Silchar, Assam, India
subhojitg@live.com

Santanu Pal
Wipro AI Research (Lab45), London, UK
santanu.pal.ju@gmail.com

Partha Pakray
NIT Silchar, Assam, India
parthapakray@gmail.com

Abstract

In today's globalized world, effective communication with people from diverse linguistic backgrounds has become increasingly crucial. While traditional methods of language translation, such as written text or voice-only translations, can accomplish the task, they often fail to capture the complete context and nuanced information conveyed through nonverbal cues like facial expressions and lip movements. In this paper, we present an end-to-end video translation system that not only translates spoken language but also synchronizes the translated speech with the lip movements of the speaker. Our system focuses on translating educational lectures in various Indian languages, and it is designed to be effective even in low-resource system settings. By incorporating lip movements that align with the target language and matching them with the speaker's voice using voice cloning techniques, our application offers an enhanced experience for students and users. This additional feature creates a more immersive and realistic learning environment, ultimately making the learning process more effective and engaging.

1 Introduction

Face-to-Face (F2F) translation is a sub-field within the research domain of Machine Translation (MT). MT refers to the process of utilizing machines to translate text or speech from one language to another (Somers, 1992). F2F translation specifically focuses on translating spoken language in real-time during face-to-face conversations or interactions. The objective is to bridge language barriers and facilitate seamless communication between individuals who speak different languages.

F2F translation is also a part of the broader field of multi-modal machine translation, which integrates videos or visual information along with translation. This approach aims to enhance engagement among native language speakers during sessions. Visual cues, such as lip synchronization according to the native languages, contribute to a more realistic and immersive translated lecture session. These visual elements provide valuable context information that aids in the translation process. Compared to image-guided multi-modal machine translation, videos provide visual and acoustic modalities with rich embedded information, such as actions, objects, and temporal transitions. From the past few years, image-based multi-modal models (Chen et al., 2022b) only had marginal performance gains compared to their text-only counterparts, although very few of them are F2F translation (Chen et al., 2022a).

F2F translation goes beyond traditional text-to-text or speech-to-speech translation methods. In a simple cascade-based F2F translation approach, several steps are involved: (i) **Capturing original speech:** the source video of a person delivering a speech is recorded or obtained, (ii) **Translating the captured speech:** the captured spoken language in the source video is translated to the desired language using machine translation techniques, (iii) **Generating an output video:** Based on the translated text, an output video is generated where the same person appears to be speaking in the translated language, and (iv) **Maintaining lip synchronization:** during the generation of the output video, efforts are made to ensure that the lip movements of the person in the video match the target language, providing lip synchronization as per the translated language. By following these steps, cascade-based F2F translation aims to deliver translated videos with synchronized lip movements, enhancing the authenticity and naturalness of the translated speech (K R et al., 2019). The intermediate steps i.e., **Translating the captured speech** can be modelled either direct (Etchegoyhen et al., 2022) or cascade-based approach (Bahar et al., 2020). The cascade-based approach first performs a speech-to-text through an automatic speech

Proceedings of the 13th International Joint Conference on Natural Language Processing and the 3rd Conference of the Asia-Pacific Chapter of the Association for Computational Linguistics: System Demonstrations, pages 1–9
November 1–4, 2023.

recognizer (ASR) then the transcribed source text to desired target text using a text-to-text machine translation system and finally a text-to-speech system transform the translated text to speech in the desired language.

In addition to managing the individual components of our cascade-based system, we face significant challenges with F2F translation, particularly in the areas of lip synchronization and voice or tone alignment. The process involves recording a speech, converting it to text using speech-to-text technologies, translating this text from the original to the target language, and then converting the translated text back to speech via text-to-speech systems. This process can be achieved using either a cascade or direct approach. A major challenge in this end-to-end F2F translation framework is ensuring that the lip movements sync with the translated speech track. This can be complex, as the duration of the translated speech may be longer or shorter than the original, depending on the distinct grammatical structures of the two languages. Additionally, the lips must move in a manner consistent with the frequency of the generated sound and must maintain the speaker's original voice or tones. Failing to do so can result in dubbing that appears off and unrealistic (Prajwal et al., 2020a).

F2F translation can have a huge impact on bridging the language gap in the educational sector. Numerous educational organisations create content to reach a global audience. Unfortunately, the lack of language intelligibility often prevents content consumers from fully utilizing the material at hand. While some videos provide manually executed dubs, these have their own set of challenges. It's true that manual translation tends to be more accurate than machine translation, but it also faces unavoidable limitations. These include cost, availability, efficiency, and most importantly, the quality of lip synchronization, which often falls short of the mark (Chung and Zisserman, 2017). Additionally, manual dubbing may be available in many but not all languages. The goal of the F2F translation system is to automate this dubbing process effectively and efficiently and make the online content available in whichever preferred language, thus overcoming the linguistic barrier between audio-visual content and the corresponding non-native consumer. This technology could also be used to assist language learning by giving students realistic and immersive opportunities to practise speaking and listening in a foreign language (Jha et al., 2019). Through this paper, we contribute to creating a more equitable and accessible education landscape that enables native individuals to learn and grow without any language barrier. Our main objective is to motivate every individual by providing a platform, through which one can grasp knowledge from videos in an unfamiliar language. To the best of our knowledge, our F2F translation framework is the first online end-to-end video translation system we bring up to the community.

2 Related Work

In this section, we present part of previous studies conducted in this field and summarise our learning and inspiration to better complement our research. Prajwal et al. (2020b) in their study explores the use of machine learning algorithms for lip-to-speech synthesis. The authors propose a new approach that takes into account individual speaking styles, resulting in increased accuracy. They use audio-visual data to train deep neural networks to capture unique lip movements and speaking styles, resulting in speech synthesis that is close to the original. The results show that their method outperforms current methods and produces speech that is similar to natural speech. K R et al. (2019) outlines a system for automatically translating speech between two people speaking different languages in real-time. The authors propose a multi-modal approach to translation that makes use of both audio and visual cues. This is accomplished by incorporating a novel visual module, LipGAN, for generating realistic talking faces in real-time from the translated audio. Their approach outperforms existing methods, demonstrating the potential for real-time F2F translation in practical applications. Ritter et al. (1999) in their research examines the development of a translation agent capable of performing real-time F2F speech translation. The authors present a multi-modal approach to translation that combines audio and visual information. They use machine learning algorithms to analyse each speaker's lip movements, speech, and facial expressions to produce a real-time audio-visual output with the speaker's face and synchronised lip movement. The results show that their method produces accurate translations and has the potential for practical applications in real-world scenarios. For translation, Chitralekha[1] is a valuable tool because it efficiently

[1]https://github.com/AI4Bharat/Chitralekha

creates multi-lingual subtitles and voice-overs for informative videos. However, it may not be a efficient for longer-length videos. Lastly, Huang et al. (2017) presented a novel problem of unpaired face translation between static photos and dynamic videos, which could be used to predict and improve video faces. To accomplish this task, the authors propose using a CycleGAN model with an identity-aware constraint. The model is trained on a large face dataset and tested on a variety of face images and videos. The results show that the proposed method can effectively translate faces between images and videos while preserving the individual's identity, outperforming existing methods.

3 The TRAVID Framework

Our framework 'TRAVID' is capable of generating translated videos from English to four Indian languages: Bengali, Hindi, Nepali, and Telugu. Flask[2] has been used as the foundation of our application, providing various built-in functionalities for building a Python-based web application. For the server-side and database, we utilize Python 3.9. In terms of audio and video processing, we primarily rely on the libraries Librosa[3] and ffmpeg[4]. These libraries provide extensive capabilities for audio and video processing, manipulation, and rendering. The primary objective of this work is to effectively and efficiently translate spoken language from an input video. Additionally, we aim to generate audio that resembles the speaker's voice and synchronize the translated speech with the speaker's lip movements. The entire process begins by obtaining the source video, target language, and speaker's gender (for voice model selection) as input from the user through our web interface. Behind the scenes, the task is divided into three sub-tasks: (1) Audio-to-Text Processing, (2) Text-to-Audio Processing, and (3) Video Processing. The steps involved in this process are depicted in Figure 1.

3.1 Audio to Text Processing

The input video, in our case an MPEG-4 (.mp4) file, is initially converted to a Waveform Audio (.wav) file using FFmpeg. This conversion enables us to perform text detection from the audio rather than the video file. Subsequently, we employ Librosa to identify non-mute sections within the 'start' and 'end' frame indexes, which are stored in a silence array. Each element of the silence array represents a small audio chunk, aiding in reducing system load and enhancing the overall efficiency of the framework during audio processing. Next, we convert each audio chunk from the silence array into an individual text chunk using Speech Recognition[5]. This library utilizes Google's Cloud speech API[6] to covert text from speech. Finally, Deep-translator[7] is employed to translate the generated text into the target language. Deep Translator utilizes the state-of-the-art Google Translate Ajax API[8] to generate the desired target language translation. The translated texts are stored and subsequently passed to the audio speech engine for further processing.

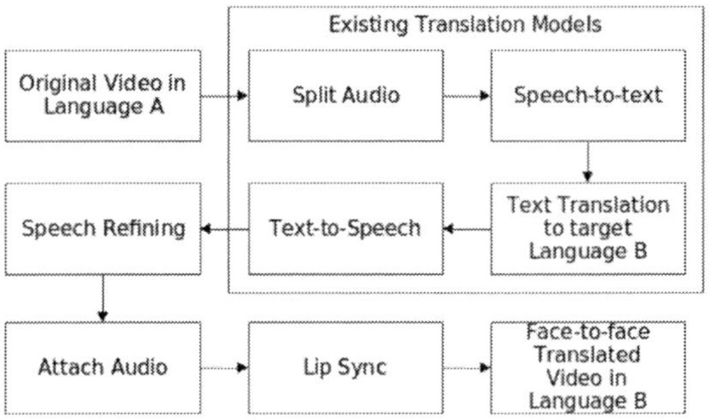

Figure 1: Steps involved in Video Translation System

3.2 Text to Audio Processing

The translated text in the target language is inserted to the gTTS[9] library, which converts the text into speech and saves it as an audio file. This marks the completion of the speech generation process and initiates the speech refinement process. In order to match the audio target length with the source audio length, adjustments are made. The length of the translated speech may differ from that of the original speech. To address this, the speech speed is modified to align with the original audio file. The "Fixed Pitch-Shifting" technique is employed to ensure that the generated speech closely resembles the voice of the original speaker. Librosa provides the capability to detect the frequency of the audio and shift the pitch of the audio time series from one musical note to another (Rosenzweig et al., 2021). In the context of voice cloning, the mean frequency of the audio is determined, with the lower note con-

[2]https://flask.palletsprojects.com/
[3]https://librosa.org/doc/latest/index.html
[4]https://pypi.org/project/ffmpeg-python/
[5]https://pypi.org/project/SpeechRecognition/
[6]www.pypi.org/project/google-cloud-speech
[7]https://pypi.org/project/deep-translator/
[8]https://pypi.org/project/googletrans/
[9]https://pypi.org/project/gTTS/

sidered as F2 (87.31 Hz) and the higher note as G6 (98.00 Hz). This frequency range represents the average range of human speech. The calculation of the steps required for shifting (n_steps) is performed using Equation 1.

$$n\_steps = \log_2(\frac{f_{src}}{f_{tgt}})^2 \quad (1)$$

The variable f_{src} refers to the frequency of the source audio and f_{tgt} refers to the corresponding target audio. With this, the Text to Audio Processing engine gives the desired audio to the video-processing engine.

3.3 Video Processing for Lip Synchronization

We have utilized a lip-synchronization network called Wav2Lip (Prajwal et al., 2020a) for the purpose of lip-syncing and generating talking face videos. This model has been trained on the LRS2 training set and demonstrates an approximate accuracy of 91% on the LRS2 test set. The video sub-network of the model examines each frame of the source video and identifies faces, with a particular focus on the lip region. The relevant audio segment is then fed into the speech sub-network component of Wav2Lip, which modifies the input face crop to emphasize the lips area and produces the final video output. Throughout this process, the lip portion of the source video is replaced by concatenating the current face crop with the lower half of the detected face. By leveraging the translated speech and the source video, Wav2Lip generates lip-synced translated videos. The resulting translated video is subsequently presented on our front-end for display.

4 Demo Scenarios

Our framework TRAVID has a visually appealing landing page[10], which has an overview of the framework (cf. Figure 2). A demonstration video of our system is available on YouTube[11]. The demo User Interface (UI) is designed a landing page, have been carefully crafted to provide a seamless and intuitive navigation experience. The landing page is effectively communicates its purpose and functionality without the need for extensive instructions or guidance. Users can easily understand what the page offers and how to navigate it intuitively. The page is organized into distinct sections that make it easy for users to locate and access the information they are looking for. This organization achieved through the use of clear headings, visually distinct sections, or a logical flow of content. The top menu bar is mentioned as a key element of the landing page, providing menu options that direct users to different feature pages. This menu bar remains accessible and visible to users across different sections of the landing page, allowing them to navigate to specific areas of interest easily. Upon signing in or signing up as a new user, the statement states that the user will be directed to the core section of the demo. This core section is the central part of the landing page, where users can access the main functionality and key features of TRAVID.

Figure 2: Homepage of TRAVID

The upload page shown in Figure 3 includes two drop-down menus: one for selecting the desired language for translation and another for choosing the output voice model (speaker). There are two options available for video input on the upload page: live recording, which allows users to capture real-time audio-visual input using their device's camera and microphone, or accepting pre-saved audio-visual content from the system. After receiving the input, the back-end framework, discussed in Section 3, initiates the translation process. Once the text, audio, and video processing are complete, the output page displays the translated video alongside the source video. Users have the option to download the source video and translated text. Additionally, they can provide reviews based on the output they received, which can help us improve and enhance the user-friendliness of our system.

The output page, depicted in Figure 4, provides a clear presentation of the original input video and the generated output video side-by-side. It offers convenient options to play and review both videos simultaneously. Additionally, users can save and download both the translated video and a translated text document. Furthermore, users can explore the demo section, which displays test case videos, to

[10] https://github.com/human71/TRAVID

[11] https://youtu.be/XNNp1xF5H0Y

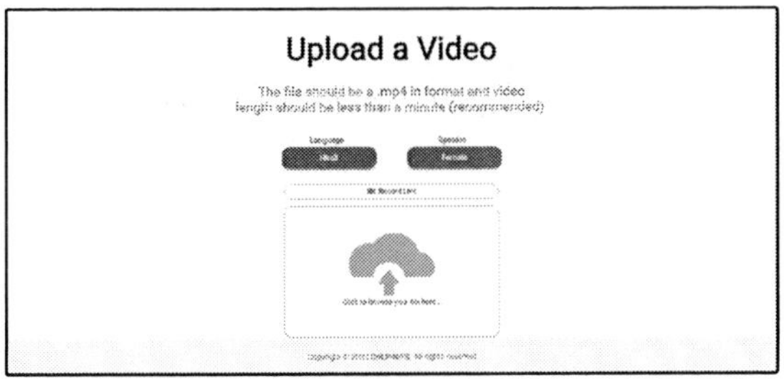

Figure 3: Upload page of TRAVID

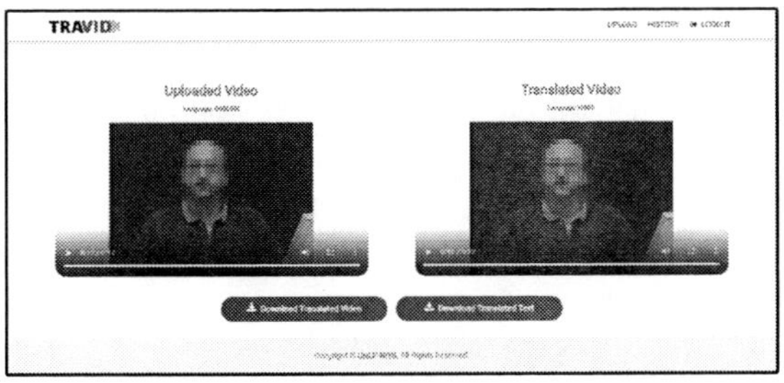

Figure 4: Output page of TRAVID

gain an understanding of the translation quality that TRAVID's translation model can produce. In addition to the demo section, TRAVID includes a feedback page where users can rate videos alongside their translated output according to specific criteria and provide feedback to enhance our framework (refer to Figure 5).

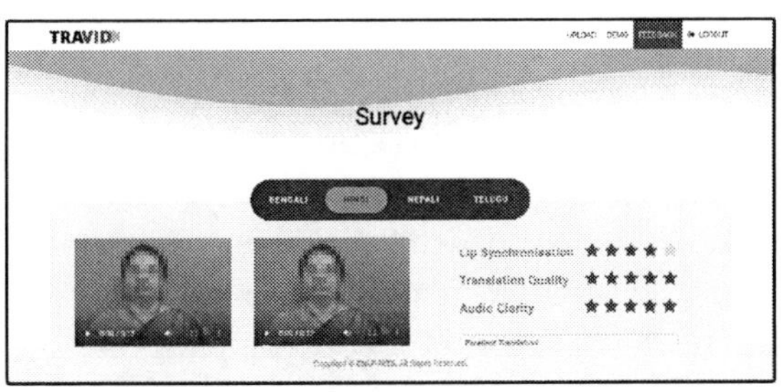

Figure 5: Survey page of TRAVID

5 Evaluation

To gauge the effectiveness of our method, We conducted a user study to assess the quality of our lip-synced translations, with participants asked to rate the translation quality, lip synchronization, and audio clarity. Evaluators compared the target video with the source language video clip and provided rankings for the quality of the output video on a scale of 1 to 5. The collected ratings were used to calculate inter-annotator agreement using Cohen's κ (Cohen, 1960), Fleiss' κ (Fleiss, 1971), and Pearson's r (Pearson, 1895) scores. Inter-annotator agreements were computed for all four languages: Bengali, Hindi, Nepali, and Telugu. Table 2 displays the agreement scores for each language based on Lip Synchronization (Lip Sync), Translation Quality (TQ), and Audio Quality (AQ). The ratings were collected by comparing the translated videos to source videos from 5 indigenous users for each of the selected languages. Moreover, a manual examination was conducted by professional evaluators, and the results are presented in Table 1. Further details regarding inter-rater agreements can be found in Appendix A, B, C.

The core component of TRAVID is based on the CNLP_NITS system, which emerged as a top performer in the Lip-Sync 2021 Challenge shared task[12]. The objective of this challenge was to convert English input videos into Hindi or Tamil output videos while ensuring lip synchronization. The quality of the Hindi Task-1 was assessed using various evaluation metrics such as Lip-Sync Quality (LSQ), Fluency Consistency (FC), Semantic Consistency (SC), and Overall User Experience (UX). Evaluators rated the quality of the output videos on a scale of 1 to 5, with higher scores indicating better quality when compared to the source language video clip. Our system, CNLP-NITS (NIT Silchar), achieved the top position with a final score of 3.84, surpassing the Baseline system (IIT Madras) with a score of 3.68 and TeamCSRL (CS RESEARCH LABS) with a score of 3.46. The comparison of the three evaluation matrices revealed a high degree of similarity. The results indicate that the translations were perceived as reasonable and easy to understand by the majority of participants, leading to fair to moderate agreement and a positive correlation among their assessments. The overall scores of the Lip-Sync Challenge 2021 are presented in Table 1.

Hindi Task 1			Hindi Task 2
CNLP_NITS	Baseline	TeamCSRL	CNLP-NITS
3.86	3.49	3.08	3.37
3.63	3.52	3.32	3.29
3.94	3.87	3.92	3.40
3.94	3.83	3.51	3.38
3.84	3.68	3.46	3.36

Table 1: Leadership Positions Based on NLP Challenges

6 Limitation

There is a constraint when uploading huge videos; the system may require a lot of computational re-

[12]Leaderboard of Lip-Sync Challenge 2021

Language	Cohen's κ			Fleiss' κ			Pearson's r		
	Lip Sync	TQ	AQ	Lip Sync	TQ	AQ	Lip Sync	TQ	AQ
Bengali	0.600	0.276	0.296	0.698	0.379	0.215	0.586	0.295	0.258
Hindi	0.510	0.390	0.391	0.595	0.291	0.345	0.400	0.292	0.318
Nepali	0.170	0.576	0.328	0.112	0.541	0.218	0.171	0.501	0.256
Telugu	0.287	0.330	0.388	0.214	0.291	0.376	0.212	0.271	0.331

Table 2: Average agreement Scores for evaluation of TRAVID generated Videos

sources and data to process and render the translated video. Also, so far we have trained our models only on a single speaker, so videos with multiple speakers may yield poor results. The quality of speech recognition and translation may vary depending on factors such as noise, accent, dialect, etc. The generated faces may not look natural or convincing enough for some applications or scenarios such as low lighting, moving background, etc. Considering the state-of-the-art ASR system in use, the ASR results were already deemed satisfactory, thus not necessitating the utilization of lip sync from the video as an additional multimodal input for accuracy enhancement. Still, the system may be unable to handle linguistic challenges such as idioms, metaphors, slang, etc. The method may not be able to capture cultural nuances and context that affect the meaning and tone of speech, as the syntheses is machine generated. The biggest bottleneck in our current system which uses cascade approach is time complexity, due to the need for extensive computation and audiovisual processing.

7 Conclusion

In this paper, we presented an end-to-end video translation system that effectively translates the speaker's native language into the local language of the audience while synchronizing the translated speech with the speaker's lip movements. Our proposed system demonstrates the potential of lip-synced Face-to-Face video translation in enhancing communication between individuals from diverse linguistic backgrounds.

Moreover, our video translation system represents a significant advancement in overcoming the limitations of traditional language translation methods. By incorporating lip synchronization and matching translated speech with the speaker's lip movements, we created an immersive and realistic experience for users. This additional feature, along with the ability to capture nonverbal cues, adds depth and context to the translated content, making it more effective and engaging, especially in educational settings.

Through our system's participation and success in the Lip-Sync 2021 Challenge, we have demonstrated its capability and superiority in achieving accurate lip synchronization and high-quality translations. The evaluations and ratings obtained from both users and professional evaluators validate the effectiveness of our approach, further emphasizing its potential for real-world applications. The positive feedback received through human assessments, as discussed in the evaluation section above, validates the effectiveness of our system. However, further research is necessary to enhance the quality of lip-syncing and explore the system's applicability in different languages and more naturalistic settings. With the ongoing advancements in technology and the increasing demand for multilingual communication, our system has the potential to revolutionize the way language translation is approached. Its adaptability to low-resource system settings makes it accessible and valuable in diverse environments.

Moving forward, we envision further enhancements and refinements to our video translation system, leveraging the advancements in natural language processing, computer vision, and machine learning. To boost video translation efficiency, the videos can be broken into smaller segments, leverage GPUs for parallel processing, batch translate frames, subsample for reduced load, and implement caching for reused translations. By continuously improving the accuracy, fluency, and naturalness of translated content, we aim to provide an unparalleled experience for users, fostering effective cross-cultural communication and knowledge sharing.

In summary, our video translation system stands as a promising solution to the challenges of multilingual communication, offering a comprehensive and immersive experience that unlocks new possibilities for global connectivity and understanding.

Ethics Statement

We honour the Code of Ethics set by IJCNLP-AACL in our paper and abide by them. We have used open-source materials in our development to produce new, better and useful resources, which will be made open-source for the keen mind to feed upon and make more improvements in the future. We have not written or in any way propagated false knowledge, hateful speech and anything controversial that may give rise to conflict. We intend good for the brighter future of mankind. We have not stolen anybody's work, and have properly cited and credited where credit is due. Our website does not feature any harmful content or advertisement. Our website is solely educational and is to be used for educational purposes only. Even though we reserve the right to use our paper and production in any way we see fit, we promise to extend them ethically and in an innovative manner.

References

Parnia Bahar, Tobias Bieschke, Ralf Schlüter, and Hermann Ney. 2020. Tight integrated end-to-end training for cascaded speech translation. *CoRR*, abs/2011.12167.

Shiyu Chen, Yawen Zeng, Da Cao, and Shaofei Lu. 2022a. Video-guided machine translation via dual-level back-translation. *Knowledge-Based Systems*, 245:108598.

Shiyu Chen, Yawen Zeng, Da Cao, and Shaofei Lu. 2022b. Vision talks: Visual relationship-enhanced transformer for video-guided machine translation. *Expert Systems with Applications*, 209:118264.

Joon Son Chung and Andrew Zisserman. 2017. Out of time: Automated lip sync in the wild. In *Computer Vision – ACCV 2016 Workshops*, pages 251–263, Cham. Springer International Publishing.

Jacob Cohen. 1960. A coefficient of agreement for nominal scales. *Educational and Psychological Measurement*, 20:37 – 46.

Thierry Etchegoyhen, Haritz Arzelus, Harritxu Gete, Aitor Alvarez, Iván G. Torre, Juan Manuel Martín-Doñas, Ander González-Docasal, and Edson Benites Fernandez. 2022. Cascade or direct speech translation? a case study. *Applied Sciences*, 12(3).

Joseph L Fleiss. 1971. Measuring nominal scale agreement among many raters. *Psychological bulletin*, 76(5):378.

Zhiwu Huang, Bernhard Kratzwald, Danda Pani Paudel, Jiqing Wu, and Luc Van Gool. 2017. Face translation between images and videos using identity-aware cyclegan. *arXiv preprint arXiv:1712.00971*.

Abhishek Jha, Vikram Voleti, Vinay Namboodiri, and C. V. Jawahar. 2019. Cross-language speech dependent lip-synchronization. In *ICASSP 2019 - 2019 IEEE International Conference on Acoustics, Speech and Signal Processing (ICASSP)*, pages 7140–7144.

Prajwal K R, Rudrabha Mukhopadhyay, Jerin Philip, Abhishek Jha, Vinay Namboodiri, and C V Jawahar. 2019. Towards automatic face-to-face translation. In *Proceedings of the 27th ACM International Conference on Multimedia*, MM '19, page 1428–1436, New York, NY, USA. Association for Computing Machinery.

Karl Pearson. 1895. Note on Regression and Inheritance in the Case of Two Parents. *Proceedings of the Royal Society of London Series I*, 58:240–242.

K R Prajwal, Rudrabha Mukhopadhyay, Vinay P. Namboodiri, and C.V. Jawahar. 2020a. A lip sync expert is all you need for speech to lip generation in the wild. In *Proceedings of the 28th ACM International Conference on Multimedia*, MM '20, page 484–492, New York, NY, USA. Association for Computing Machinery.

KR Prajwal, Rudrabha Mukhopadhyay, Vinay P Namboodiri, and CV Jawahar. 2020b. Learning individual speaking styles for accurate lip to speech synthesis. In *Proceedings of the IEEE/CVF Conference on Computer Vision and Pattern Recognition*, pages 13796–13805.

Max Ritter, Uwe Meier, Jie Yang, and Alex Waibel. 1999. Face translation: A multimodal translation agent. In *AVSP'99-International Conference on Auditory-Visual Speech Processing*.

Sebastian Rosenzweig, Simon Schwär, Jonathan Driedger, and Meinard Müller. 2021. Adaptive pitch-shifting with applications to intonation adjustment in a cappella recordings. In *2021 24th International Conference on Digital Audio Effects (DAFx)*, pages 121–128. IEEE.

Harold Somers. 1992. An introduction to machine translation.

A Cohen's Kappa

The definition of κ is

$$\kappa = \frac{p_o - p_e}{1 - p_e}$$

where p_o denotes the relative observed agreement among raters and p_e denotes the hypothetical probability of chance agreement, calculated by using observed data to compute the odds of each observer randomly seeing each group.

B Fleiss' Kappa

The Fleiss' kappa κ can be defined as,

$$\kappa = \frac{\bar{P} - \bar{P}_e}{1 - \bar{P}_e}$$

The factors $1 - \bar{P}_e$ and $\bar{P} - \bar{P}_e$ indicate the level of agreement that can be reached above chance and the level of agreement that has actually been attained.

C Pearson Correlation Coefficient Analysis

Given a pair of random variables (X, Y), the formula for ρ is:

$$\rho_{X,Y} = \frac{cov(X, Y)}{\sigma_X \sigma_Y}$$

where cov is the covariance, σ_X is the standard deviation of X and σ_Y is the standard deviation of Y.

Table [3, 4, 5] displays the calculated Pearson Correlation Coefficient (PCC) values for Bengali, Table [6, 7, 8] displays the calculated PCC values for Hindi, Table [9, 10, 11] displays the calculated PCC values for Nepali, Table [12, 13, 14] displays the calculated PCC values for Telugu with respect to all three assessment areas, namely Lip Synchronization, Translation Quality, and Audio Quality. Where R1-R5 (Rater 01-05) denote five raters who assessed our system in all four languages.

	R1	R2	R3	R4	R5
R1	1	-0.2	0.81	0.72	0.46
R2	-0.2	1	0.75	0.81	0.85
R3	0.81	0.75	1	0.84	-0.02
R4	0.72	0.55	0.84	1	0.84
R5	0.46	0.85	-0.02	0.84	1

Table 3: PCC for Bengali Lip Synchronization

	R1	R2	R3	R4	R5
R1	1	0.32	0.86	0.21	0.87
R2	0.32	1	0.68	0.12	0.38
R3	0.86	0.68	1	-0.64	0.57
R4	0.21	0.12	-0.64	1	-0.42
R5	0.87	0.38	0.57	-0.42	1

Table 4: PCC for Bengali Translation Quality

	R1	R2	R3	R4	R5
R1	1	0.79	-0.18	0.25	0.33
R2	0.79	1	0.42	0.39	0.12
R3	-0.18	0.42	1	-0.19	0.39
R4	0.25	0.39	-0.19	1	0.26
R5	0.33	0.12	0.39	0.26	1

Table 5: PCC for Bengali Audio Quality

	R1	R2	R3	R4	R5
R1	1	-0.12	0.26	-0.06	0.21
R2	-0.12	1	0.55	0.39	0.65
R3	0.26	0.55	1	0.66	0.72
R4	-0.06	0.39	0.66	1	0.74
R5	0.21	0.65	0.72	0.74	1

Table 6: PCC for Hindi Lip Synchronization

	R1	R2	R3	R4	R5
R1	1	-0.42	-0.42	0.51	0.66
R2	-0.42	1	0.88	0.56	-0.12
R3	0.36	0.88	1	0.76	0.62
R4	0.51	0.56	0.76	1	-0.11
R5	0.66	-0.12	0.62	-0.11	1

Table 7: PCC for Hindi Translation Quality

	R1	R2	R3	R4	R5
R1	1	0.22	0.68	-0.01	0.72
R2	0.22	1	-0.19	0.3	0.59
R3	0.68	-0.19	1	0.12	0.26
R4	-0.01	0.3	0.12	1	0.49
R5	0.72	0.59	0.26	0.49	1

Table 8: PCC for Hindi Audio Quality

	R1	R2	R3	R4	R5
R1	1	-0.2	-0.01	0.52	0.11
R2	-0.2	1	0.16	0.29	0.21
R3	-0.01	0.16	1	-0.22	0.34
R4	0.52	0.29	-0.22	1	0.51
R5	0.11	0.21	0.34	0.51	1

Table 9: PCC for Nepali Lip Synchronization

	R1	R2	R3	R4	R5
R1	1	0.69	0.58	-0.09	0.66
R2	0.69	1	0.49	0.63	-0.21
R3	0.58	0.49	1	0.66	0.79
R4	-0.09	0.63	0.66	1	0.81
R5	0.66	-0.21	0.79	0.81	1

Table 10: PCC for Nepali Translation Quality

	R1	R2	R3	R4	R5
R1	1	0.11	-0.02	-0.15	0.29
R2	0.11	1	0.59	0.63	0.82
R3	-0.02	0.59	1	0.26	-0.09
R4	-0.15	0.63	0.26	1	0.12
R5	0.29	0.82	-0.09	0.12	1

Table 11: PCC for Nepali Audio Quality

	R1	R2	R3	R4	R5
R1	1	0.19	0.26	-0.02	-0.16
R2	0.19	1	-0.05	0.19	0.22
R3	0.26	-0.05	1	0.39	0.51
R4	-0.02	0.19	0.39	1	0.59
R5	-0.16	0.22	0.51	0.59	1

Table 12: PCC for Telugu Lip Synchronization

	R1	R2	R3	R4	R5
R1	1	-0.18	-0.18	0.44	-0.13
R2	-0.18	1	0.63	0.31	0.58
R3	0.39	0.63	1	0.58	0.67
R4	0.44	0.31	0.58	1	-0.01
R5	-0.13	0.58	0.67	-0.01	1

Table 13: PCC for Telugu Translation Quality

	R1	R2	R3	R4	R5
R1	1	0.83	0.11	0.32	0.19
R2	0.83	1	0.59	0.3	0.63
R3	0.11	0.59	1	-0.19	0.61
R4	0.32	0.41	0.3	1	-0.08
R5	0.19	0.63	0.61	-0.08	1

Table 14: PCC for Telugu Audio Quality

CustodiAI: A System for Predicting Child Custody Outcomes

Yining Juan,[1] **Chung-Chi Chen,**[2] **Hsin-Hsi Chen,**[1] **Daw-Wei Wang**[3,4]
[1] Department of Computer Science and Information Engineering,
National Taiwan University, Taiwan
[2] AIST, Japan
[3] Department of Physics, National Tsing Hua University, Taiwan
[4] Center for the Applications and Developments of AI in Humanity and Social Sciences,
National Tsing Hua University, Taiwan
ynjuan@nlg.csie.ntu.edu.tw, c.c.chen@acm.org
hhchen@csie.ntu.edu.tw , dwwang@phys.nthu.edu.tw

Abstract

Predicting child custody decisions post-divorce is crucial but challenging due to numerous non-numerical, text-based factors, particularly in joint custody scenarios. This study presents the Intermediate Self-Supervised Training (ISST) method, a two-stage approach that classifies document paragraphs using original rationale labels before leveraging this to predict custody at the document level. Achieving up to 90.57% accuracy and notably, a 78.95% F1-score for joint custody cases, it surpasses previous models by 13%. We further refine the model to mitigate gender bias in the training data and provide error estimations, enhancing fairness and reliability. Our user-friendly online system exemplifies our model's applicability in out-of-court dispute resolution, potentially reducing time and financial strains for families in crisis.

1 Introduction

The principle of "best interests of the minor child" serves as the keystone of judicial decision-making in post-divorce custody matters. Nonetheless, the definition and interpretation of this standard are fraught with complexity. For example, Article 1055-1 of Taiwan's Civil Code,[1] which requires judges to factor in the parent's commitment and aptitude for the child's protection and education when determining custody. This, and similar statements found in the Civil Code, are laden with unstructured, descriptive human language that makes precise prediction of judicial outcomes a challenging endeavor.

The predictive challenge escalates when it comes to joint custody awards, a vital yet relatively uncommon outcome in legal proceedings. Deciding on sole custody—whether to grant it to the mother or father—translates into a binary classification problem, where it's feasible to determine which party is best suited for the child's welfare, both theoretically and practically. Conversely, real-world scenarios often entertain the possibility of joint custody, which introduces a more complex ternary classification task in machine learning terms. Neglecting this dimension could result in overlooking crucial factors when evaluating the child's best interest, consequently rendering the model ineffective for practical applications.

This work aims to devise a predictive machine learning model that leverages the nuance and depth of human language rationale, thus enhancing the efficiency of public dispute resolution. We propose the Intermediate Self-Supervised Training (ISST) method, built on expert-labeled training data, which incorporates a two-stage training process for custody's ternary classification. In our model, we've integrated 13 custody factors to bolster its explainability for the public. The model's overall accuracy peaks at 90.57%, and in cases involving joint custody, it attains an F_1-score as high as 78.95%, marking a 13% increase from previous models. Keeping in view the ethical implications of system deployment, we've also incorporated data augmentation and model error estimation to mitigate potential gender bias and avoid misinterpretation of predicted results. A user-friendly online demo landing page is available[2], offering users the option to select inputs in either text format, categorical items, or both. By significantly reducing the time and financial costs tied to legal processes, our work offers a promising tool for out-of-court dispute resolution.

2 Related Work

Over recent decades, the rise of Artificial Intelligence (AI) applications has instigated transformative changes in all facets of human existence. One such significantly impacted area is the judi-

[1] https://is.gd/VDimZk

[2] CustodiAI: https://demo-cjdp-aifr.herokuapp.com/demo-home

Proceedings of the 13th International Joint Conference on Natural Language Processing and the 3rd Conference of the Asia-Pacific Chapter of the Association for Computational Linguistics: System Demonstrations, pages 10–16
November 1–4, 2023.

cial sector, where researchers can leverage the vast corpus of high-quality data from court judgments to train ML models. Numerous studies have investigated applications utilizing data from legal decisions across different countries (Sulea et al., 2017; Luo et al., 2017; Kowsrihawat et al., 2018; Malik et al., 2021). In most of these applications, experts have labeled the data sources using either categorical or numerical variables.

While initial AI explorations in the judicial realm focused mainly on criminal cases, recent trends indicate a broader scope. This includes the adoption of Natural Language Processing (NLP) techniques to analyze verdicts, exemplified by studies on judgments from the European Court of Human Rights (Aletras et al., 2016), and later refined in subsequent works (Medvedeva et al., 2018). Furthermore, efforts by researchers like Chen & Eagel have contributed specialized datasets for unique contexts such as asylum adjudication (Chen and Eagel, 2017).

Despite the progress made in the field, Legal Judgment Prediction (LJP) faces several challenges, including the issue of AI model predictions' asymmetry in distinguishing positive and negative outcomes (Valvoda et al., 2023). This discrepancy is prevalent even with the emergence of models that simulate real-world court processes and human judge decision-making, indicating the complexity of the problem. Notably, models utilizing supervised contrastive learning frameworks have demonstrated their ability to differentiate between similar law articles and charges, mirroring the analytical skills of real-world judges (Zhang et al., 2023). However, there are still concerns regarding the occasional shortcomings of LJP models, particularly in accurately identifying nuanced critical events (Feng et al., 2022). To address this issue, the Event-based Prediction Model (EPM) focuses on capturing detailed information about specific events, providing a potential solution to enhance the performance of LJP models (Feng et al., 2022).

Our research focuses on analyzing child custody outcomes within the field of family law. While models developed by Long et al. show promising results when applied to carefully curated divorce datasets (Long et al., 2019), they may struggle to capture the complexities of real-world situations. Predicting court judgment outcomes, particularly in cases involving child custody, is a complex endeavor. The diverse range of potential outcomes, including shared custody arrangements and sole custody allocations, adds an additional layer of intricacy to the prediction process. This multifaceted landscape presents challenges when it comes to deploying machine learning models in public domains.

The significance of predicting legal outcomes extends beyond academic realms. As our research demonstrates, there is a critical demand for accurate prediction models, particularly in intricate situations such as post-divorce child custody. To address this need, we propose the implementation of the Intermediate Self-Supervised Training (ISST) method. This approach aims to enhance the reliability, fairness, and robustness of custody outcome predictions.

3 Data Preparation

We sourced court verdicts for this study from the Open Data of Taiwan Judicial Yuan(Taiwan Judicial Yuan, 2018), spanning January 1, 2015, to December 31, 2017. Using three keywords: "divorce", "discretion", and "the best interests of the child", we filtered unrelated verdicts, yielding a collection of 1,343 cases related to post-divorce child custody. After expert manual examination and labeling, we identified 529 cases where both parents sought custody. The court judgments fell into three categories: sole custody to the plaintiff (252 cases), sole custody to the defendant (184 cases), and joint custody (93 cases). We used 'plaintiff' and 'defendant' instead of 'father' and 'mother' to avoid potential gender bias in the data.

3.1 Rationale Paragraphs

Court judgment rationales, derived solely from the judge-authored text in verdicts, were labeled and classified into four categories related to custody decisions: "favorable to plaintiff (FP)", "unfavorable to the plaintiff (UP)", "favorable to defendant (FD)", and "unfavorable to the defendant (UD)". Each rationale ranged from 20 to 200 Chinese characters. Importantly, to avoid potential gender biases, plaintiffs' and defendants' genders were not labeled in the dataset. Below are examples of the four types of paragraphs labeled in our dataset:

(1) An FP rationale:

The plaintiff has stable parenting capacities, parenting time, a caring environment, educational planning, and a high motivation to obtain custody.

(2) A UP rationale:

The plaintiff, during this marital relationship, was incarcerated due to drug charges during pregnancy, which indicates an improper parental attitude and inability to provide a stable and positive child-raising environment.

(3) An FD rationale:

The child has resided with the defendant for an extended period without any negative circumstances in the living environment and parental support system.

(4) A UD rationale:

The defendant is employed as a university lecturer and also teaches a baking class, resulting in a weaker parental bond due to the distant family relationship.

In this study, we have labeled 4,153 paragraphs, encompassing 1,637 paragraphs favorable to the plaintiff, 423 unfavorable to the plaintiff, 1,475 favorable to the defendant, and 618 unfavorable to the defendant.

3.2 Custody Factors

In addition to the rationale paragraphs, we labeled 13 factors relevant to custody decisions. These factors, derived from Article 1055-1 of the Civil Code in Taiwan and previous studies, include: (1) Child's Age, (2) Child's Willingness, (3) Child's Development, (4) Parent's Occupation, (5) Parent's Financial Status, (6) Parent's Health Status, (7) Parent's Character, (8) Parent's Living Condition, (9) Primary Caregiver, (10) Parent's Willingness and Capability, (11) Parent's Friendliness to the Other Parent, (12) Parent-Child Affection, (13) Supporting System.

Upon examining all the verdicts in our dataset, we found that almost all the factors mentioned by judges regarding child custody decisions could be classified into the aforementioned 13 factors. For instance, the sample FP paragraph provided in the previous subsection could also be labeled by Parent's Willingness and Capability. Notably, there were cases where a paragraph was labeled with more than one factor due to the complex descriptions in verdicts.

4 System Description

The backbone of our system is the ISST model, a two-stage BERT-based model used for predicting child custody. The initial stage is a self-supervised training stage using rationale labels for paragraph classification, followed by the second stage, which is supervised fine-tuning on our target task. This stage utilizes the encoder weights produced by the initial stage. Figure 1 compares our approach with previous methods.

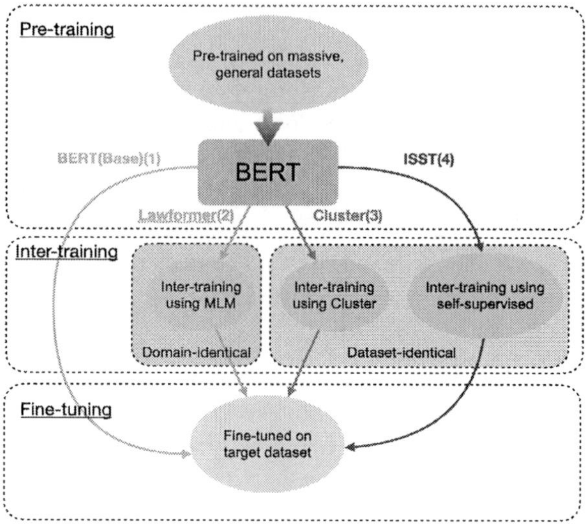

Figure 1: The diagram shows the different stages involved in developing a pre-trained model. During the pre-training phase, the model is trained on general corpora. In the inter-training phase, the Lawformer(Xiao et al., 2021) (illustrated in Path 2 of the figure) is introduced to data specific to the target domain and is trained to employ the Masked Language Model (MLM) approach. On the other hand, the method advanced by Shnarch, Eyal, et al. (Shnarch et al., 2022) (represented in Path 3 of the figure) as well as our proposed ISST(path 4 of the figure) exclusively utilize the dataset associated with the target task, devoid of data from other related domains, focusing on classification tasks.

4.1 First Stage: Intermediate Self-Supervised Training

Fine-tuning pre-trained BERT (Kenton and Toutanova, 2019) word vectors is a standard practice for contemporary NLP tasks. However, performance can vary greatly for task-specific datasets. To improve prediction accuracy for judicial decisions regarding child custody, we propose a self-supervised, intermediate task training method that aligns learned features more closely with our final goal.

While BERT's pre-trained word vectors are generalized, they may not be sufficiently precise for specialized tasks. We convert the original input features into an intermediate training target, enabling the model to learn representations more relevant to the task at hand. Although the accuracy of the final task can be enhanced through a supervised learning method with different data (Gururangan et al., 2020) or an unsupervised learning method (Shnarch et al., 2022), these approaches do not correlate strongly with the final task.

In contrast, our method involves training rationale paragraphs to be classified by their inherent attributes (Favorable or Unfavorable), which are highly correlated with the target task sentences, albeit not identical. In the first stage of training, it's crucial to ensure a balanced proportion of 'Favorable' and 'Unfavorable' rationale paragraphs. An imbalance in the dataset can introduce biases during the intermediate fine-tuning, which might adversely affect the subsequent target task fine-tuning. Then, the encoder weights thus obtained are used for the target task, which is the ternary classification of child custody using "effective verdicts". This intermediate task training is essentially a self-supervised learning approach that maps the input data (rationale paragraphs) onto the intrinsic attributes of the "effective verdicts". However, these attributes, despite their high correlation, might not yield optimal results when directly applied to predict child custody. As such, we leverage the resulting embedding weights of the rationale paragraphs instead of the original BERT word vectors for the second training stage.

4.2 Second Stage: Target Task Fine-Tuning

In the second stage, we add an initialized classifier layer on top of the BERT model, well-trained from the previous stage. We structure the input data as: $D = \{(p^{(FP)}, p^{(UP)}, p^{(FD)}, p^{(UD)})_i, y_i\}_{i=1}^N$, corresponding to rationale paragraphs Favorable to the Plaintiff (FP), Unfavorable to the Plaintiff (UP), Favorable to the Defendant (FD), and Unfavorable to the Defendant (UD). This input tuple is then mapped onto one of three judicial decision outcomes: $y \in \{Plaintiff, Defendant, BothParties\}$.

To utilize the cross-attention module in BERT, facilitating the fusion of fine-grained information within the paragraphs and their rationale and factor labels, we design the following prompt for each input item p_i^j with $j \in \{FP, UP, FD, UD\}$ to the BERT model:

$$p_i^j = \text{[CLS] } f_i^j \text{ [SEP] } r_i^j \text{ [SEP]}.$$

In this formulation, r_i^j represents the rationale paragraph favorable/unfavorable to the plaintiff/defendant, and f_i^j follows the form: "The party has [Sentiment] factors for [Factors]". The "Factors" slot is populated with Chinese words describing previously mentioned factors such as Child's Age or Primary Caregiver, and the "Sentiment" slot is populated with Chinese words that represent "Favorable" or "Unfavorable".

This prompt significantly enhances the user interface's flexibility: users can decide their preferred input style— rationale text only,r_i^j, itemized factors only,f_i^j, or keeps both r_i^j and f_i^j as input. We also augment only factors or rationale text data during the training phase, so that the model can support these three different inputs at the same time.

However, it's worth noting that the longest input sequence length accepted by $BERT_{BASE}$ is only 512 tokens. The total length of the inputs $p^{(FP)}, p^{(UP)}, p^{(FD)}, p^{(UD)}$ averages around 2549 tokens, meaning direct concatenation would result in a significant loss of valuable information. To circumvent this, we propose an iterative solution for this long text problem, as detailed in Algorithm 1: we process the four input items ($p^{(FP)}$, etc.) in sequence through BERT, obtaining their respective [CLS] embedding vectors of 768 dimensions. These embeddings are concatenated into a 3072-dimension ($= 768 \times 4$) vector representing the "effective verdict", which is then fed into the neural network classifier to produce the final prediction for child custody.

Algorithm 1 ISST algorithm

```
Input: ({p^(FP), p^(UP), p^(FD), p^(UD)}, y)
Output: Θ
Θ ← Pre-trained from inter-training method.
V = {}
for each ({p^(FP), p^(UP), p^(FD), p^(UD)}, y) do
    for j = {FP, UP, FD, UD} do
        V = V ⊕ BatchNorm(BERT(p^j))
    end for
    Obtain the predicted result
    ŷ = argmin_{y*} ℓ(y*|V)
    Update the network via the gradient
    ∇_G L((y*|V))
end for
```

5 Evaluation

In this section, we employ a 5-fold cross-validation approach to compare the performance of our ISST method with three other methods. Figure 1 highlights the differences among these techniques. The first method is the standard $BERT$(Kenton and Toutanova, 2019) model, which relies only on pre-trained encoder weights and excludes intermediate training. The second method, Lawformer(Xiao

	Sole Custody (Binary)			Sole Custody & Joint Custody (Three Categories)			
	Accuracy	$F_1(P)$	$F_1(D)$	Accuracy	$F_1(P)$	$F_1(D)$	$F_1(B)$
BERT	95.91±1.54	96.53±1.41	94.93±1.68	83.77±4.48	92.73±1.75	85.24±5.15	53.12±10.55
Lawformer	94.55±0.85	95.35±0.92	93.29±0.84	85.38±4.36	92.06±2.37	89.25±4.95	51.94±10.64
Cluster	97.73±1.44	98.02±1.28	97.3±1.72	85.85±3.3	95.74±1.62	84.62±6.01	65.00±3.77
ISST (Proposed)	**98.85±2.43**	**99.18±2.1**	**98.63±2.89**	**90.57±3.07**	**95.83±1.71**	**89.74±3.69**	**78.95±7.7**

Table 1: Experimental results under different task settings.

et al., 2021), involves intermediate training with Masked Language Model (MLM) tasks before fine-tuning. The third method, Cluster (Shnarch et al., 2022), employs an intermediate unsupervised learning approach for training.

Our analysis begins with the prediction results for sole custody cases, which involve binary classification, with custody awarded either to the Plaintiff or the Defendant. For these predictions, we utilize both rationale paragraphs and custody factors as input features. As Table 1 illustrates, our ISST approach demonstrates superior performance in terms of accuracy (Acc.) and F_1-scores for both Plaintiff ($F_1(P)$) and Defendant ($F_1(D)$).

Table 1 extends the comparison to include cases involving both sole custody and joint custody. This extends the problem to a ternary classification task, with custody awarded to the plaintiff, to the defendant, or to both parties. Our ISST model's overall accuracy exceeds 90%, outperforming all other models by at least 5%. When comparing the F_1-scores of the three classes, our model again secures the highest scores. The most significant difference, exceeding 27%, is observed in the cases of joint custody. This demonstrates that our ISST model significantly improves the prediction of child custody when joint custody is a potential outcome.

It is important to note that we also modified the task of Intermediate Self-Supervised Training (ISST) from determining the favorability or unfavorability of a rationale paragraph to identifying the specific custody factor to which the paragraph relates among the 13 available factors. Following this modification, we observed a decline in the performance of the ISST (specifically, the accuracy for predictions related to Sole Custody & Joint Custody was 83.46%, which is similar to the baseline performance achieved by simply fine-tuning BERT). This outcome aligns with the fact that when judges make custody rulings, they address the favorable/unfavorable conditions much more than which custody factors presented by each party in a holistic manner for their final decision.

This instructive result indicates that the purpose of the intermediate task should be to serve as a bridge between the pre-trained BERT and the distinct objectives of the target task. By integrating a task with a high correlation to the target during intermediate training, the expressiveness of BERT for the target task can be enhanced. Therefore, the careful selection of a task with a higher correlation to the target task for ISST is pivotal to optimizing the performance of the target task.

6 System

6.1 Ethical Considerations for System Deployment

Before deploying our ISST model, trained on real-world cases for public use, it's crucial to address potential ethical issues, particularly gender bias. Our labels "plaintiff" and "defendant", rather than "father" and "mother", might imply gender neutrality, but our dataset of 529 cases shows imbalance: fathers filed 42.34% and mothers 57.66% of the cases. Since only 19.64% of fathers and 68.20% of mothers were granted sole custody, gender bias may unintentionally manifest in our model.

To counter this, we've augmented the data by interchanging plaintiffs and defendants' features and outcomes in sole custody cases, creating a larger, gender-balanced dataset. Consequently, our *balanced* ISST model retains its accuracy while reducing the potential gender bias, enhancing its public application reliability.

In addition, We've also integrated an error estimation method using token-level perturbations on rationale statements, repeated 100 times on 5 differently seeded models. This yields 500 predictions, the standard deviation of which indicates prediction reliability. It is interesting to find that dominant probabilities (P>80%) typically have minimal errors (<5%), whereas tight contests (P<50%) show larger errors (>24%), suggesting users either provide additional information or ignore results. To offer users a more intuitive understanding of the trustworthiness of a given prediction, we trans-

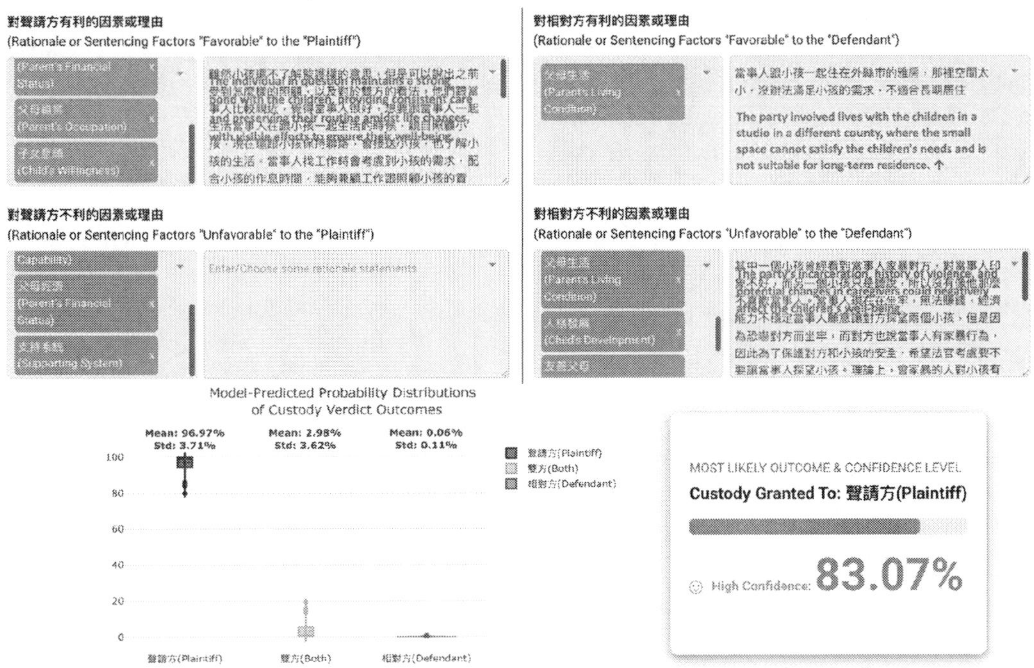

Figure 2: Screenshot of the proposed CustodiAI.

late this error estimation into a confidence value (0-1) using the formula $confidence = e^{-k*std}$. Based on our tests, we classify confidence values above 77.88% as 'high', below 30.11% as 'low', and those in between as 'moderate'.[3]

This adaptive adjustment helps avoid user misinterpretation of our system's outputs, boosting its trustworthiness and paving its way as a reliable AI solution for public use.

6.2 Demonstration

In this section, we showcase the functionality of the Intermediate Self-Supervised Training (ISST) system. Figure 2 shows the screenshot of the proposed CustodiAI. Additional details can be found in the accompanying demo video[4].

To simplify the user experience, we allow inputs of either rational statements or relevant custody factors. Sample statements based on court rulings are provided to help users articulate their cases effectively. Users can then select and adjust these templates to best fit their circumstances.

Contrary to most other comparable systems that only offer a single most probable result, our interface displays a violin plot of 500 predictions, indicating possible outcomes and their associated error estimations. A summary of the most probable judgment and its confidence level is displayed at the bottom right.

By pairing visually engaging prediction distributions with confidence scores, we can empower users to make informed decisions. The interactive interface's simplicity and flexibility deepen understanding of AI predictions, fostering trust and engagement. This approach helps offset possible model bias, reinforcing our system as a reliable public tool.

7 Conclusion

Our study introduces the novel Intermediate Self-Supervised Training (ISST) method for predicting complex child custody decisions, significantly improving upon previous models with an accuracy up to 90.57% and an F1-score of 78.95% in joint custody cases. We've ensured fairness and reliability by mitigating gender bias in the training data and providing error estimations for the predicted results. This work offers a tangible, user-friendly solution for out-of-court dispute resolution, marking a significant stride towards more efficient, accurate, and fair decision-making in child custody disputes.

[3]We empirically chose k=5 in the formula $confidence = e^{-k*std}$ to accentuate differences within the most common standard deviation range (0-0.24) in the testing dataset. Confidence thresholds of 30.11% and 77.88% were defined based on the confidence scores calculated from the first (q1) and third (q3) standard deviation quartiles, respectively, to delineate low, moderate, and high confidence levels.

[4]Demo video: https://reurl.cc/leo9AV

Acknowledgments

We thank Prof. Yun-Hsien Diana Lin, Yun-Diao Lin, Ya-Lun Li and Hong-Hsiang Liu at National Tsing Hua University for the annotation of court verdicts and important discussion. This research is partially supported by the National Science and Technology Council, Taiwan, under grants MOST 109-2420-H-007-012-, MOST 109-2634-F-007-011-, MOST 110-2634-F-007-020-, MOST 110-2221-E-002-128-MY3 and NSTC 111-2634-F-002-023-. Yining Juan and Daw-Wei Wang were also supported by National Tsing Hua University through the Higher Education Sprout Project by the Ministry of Education(MOE) in Taiwan. The work of Chung-Chi Chen was supported in part by JSPS KAKENHI Grant Number 23K16956 and a project JPNP20006, commissioned by the New Energy and Industrial Technology Development Organization (NEDO).

Limitations

The limitation of our method stays in the form of the original data: it has to contain rationale paragraphs with proper inner attribute labeling so that the intermediate self-supervised training can be applied. This type of input feature may not be available for other types of text and hence limits the application of our model. Furthermore, since these rationale paragraphs are originally written by judges, layman users of our system may not be able to generate the same type of writing for their input information, reducing the accuracy of the custody prediction when applied to the public.

References

Nikolaos Aletras, Dimitrios Tsarapatsanis, Daniel Preoţiuc-Pietro, and Vasileios Lampos. 2016. Predicting judicial decisions of the european court of human rights: A natural language processing perspective. *PeerJ Computer Science*, 2:e93.

Daniel L Chen and Jess Eagel. 2017. Can machine learning help predict the outcome of asylum adjudications? In *Proceedings of the 16th edition of the International Conference on Articial Intelligence and Law*, pages 237–240.

Yi Feng, Chuanyi Li, and Vincent Ng. 2022. Legal judgment prediction via event extraction with constraints. In *Proceedings of the 60th Annual Meeting of the Association for Computational Linguistics (Volume 1: Long Papers)*, pages 648–664.

Suchin Gururangan, Ana Marasović, Swabha Swayamdipta, Kyle Lo, Iz Beltagy, Doug Downey, and Noah A Smith. 2020. Don't stop pretraining: Adapt language models to domains and tasks. *arXiv preprint arXiv:2004.10964*.

Jacob Devlin Ming-Wei Chang Kenton and Lee Kristina Toutanova. 2019. Bert: Pre-training of deep bidirectional transformers for language understanding. In *Proceedings of naacL-HLT*, volume 1, page 2.

Kankawin Kowsrihawat, Peerapon Vateekul, and Prachya Boonkwan. 2018. Predicting judicial decisions of criminal cases from thai supreme court using bi-directional gru with attention mechanism. In *2018 5th Asian Conference on Defense Technology (ACDT)*, pages 50–55. IEEE.

Shangbang Long, Cunchao Tu, Zhiyuan Liu, and Maosong Sun. 2019. Automatic judgment prediction via legal reading comprehension. In *Chinese Computational Linguistics: 18th China National Conference*, pages 558–572. Springer.

Bingfeng Luo, Yansong Feng, Jianbo Xu, Xiang Zhang, and Dongyan Zhao. 2017. Learning to predict charges for criminal cases with legal basis. *arXiv preprint arXiv:1707.09168*.

Vijit Malik, Rishabh Sanjay, Shubham Kumar Nigam, Kripa Ghosh, Shouvik Kumar Guha, Arnab Bhattacharya, and Ashutosh Modi. 2021. Ildc for cjpe: Indian legal documents corpus for court judgment prediction and explanation. *arXiv preprint arXiv:2105.13562*.

Masha Medvedeva, Michel Vols, and Martijn Wieling. 2018. Judicial decisions of the european court of human rights: Looking into the crystal ball. In *Proceedings of the conference on empirical legal studies*, page 24.

Eyal Shnarch, Ariel Gera, Alon Halfon, Lena Dankin, Leshem Choshen, Ranit Aharonov, and Noam Slonim. 2022. Cluster & tune: Boost cold start performance in text classification. *arXiv preprint arXiv:2203.10581*.

Octavia-Maria Sulea, Marcos Zampieri, Mihaela Vela, and Josef Van Genabith. 2017. Predicting the law area and decisions of french supreme court cases. *arXiv preprint arXiv:1708.01681*.

Josef Valvoda, Ryan Cotterell, and Simone Teufel. 2023. On the role of negative precedent in legal outcome prediction. *Transactions of the Association for Computational Linguistics*, 11:34–48.

Chaojun Xiao, Xueyu Hu, Zhiyuan Liu, Cunchao Tu, and Maosong Sun. 2021. Lawformer: A pre-trained language model for chinese legal long documents. *AI Open*, 2:79–84.

Han Zhang, Zhicheng Dou, Yutao Zhu, and Ji-Rong Wen. 2023. Contrastive learning for legal judgment prediction. *ACM Transactions on Information Systems*, 41(4):1–25.

Turning Whisper into Real-Time Transcription System

Dominik Macháček[1] and **Raj Dabre**[2] and **Ondřej Bojar**[1]

Charles University, Faculty of Mathematics and Physics,
Institute of Formal and Applied Linguistics[1]

National Institute of Information and Communications Technology, Kyoto, Japan[2]
[1]{machacek,bojar}@ufal.mff.cuni.cz, [2]raj.dabre@nict.go.jp

Abstract

Whisper is one of the recent state-of-the-art multilingual speech recognition and translation models, however, it is not designed for real time transcription. In this paper, we build on top of Whisper and create **Whisper-Streaming**, an implementation of real-time speech transcription and translation of Whisper-like models. Whisper-Streaming uses local agreement policy with self-adaptive latency to enable streaming transcription. We show that Whisper-Streaming achieves high quality and 3.3 seconds latency on unsegmented long-form speech transcription test set, and we demonstrate its robustness and practical usability as a component in live transcription service at a multilingual conference.

1 Introduction

Whisper (Radford et al., 2022) is a recent state-of-the-art system for automatic speech recognition (ASR) for 97 languages and for translation from 96 languages into English. Whisper models are publicly available under the MIT license. However, the current public implementations of Whisper inference usually allow only offline processing of audio documents that are completely available at the time of processing, without any processing time constraints.

Real-time streaming mode is useful in certain situations, e.g. for live captioning. It means that the source speech audio has to be processed at the time when it is being recorded. The transcripts or translations have to be delivered with a short additive latency, e.g. in 2 seconds. There are some implementations of Whisper for streaming, but their approach is rather naive, they e.g. first record a 30-second audio segment, and then process it. The latency of these methods is large, and the quality on the segment boundaries is low because a simple content unaware segmentation can split a word in the middle.

In this work, we implement, evaluate and demonstrate Whisper in simultaneous streaming mode using the simple but effective LocalAgreement (Liu et al., 2020) algorithm. LocalAgreement is one particular streaming policy that can be used to convert any full-sequence to full-sequence model to operate in simultaneous streaming mode. It was used by the winning system CUNI-KIT at IWSLT 2022 simultaneous speech translation shared task (Polák et al., 2022). We call our implementation **Whisper-Streaming**, although it is applicable to any model with API similar to Whisper. According to our evaluation, it achieves 3.3 seconds latency on average for English ASR on the European Parliament speech test set ESIC (Macháček et al., 2021), when running on NVIDIA A40 GPU, a fast hardware processing unit. We test it also on German and Czech ASR and present the results and suggestions for the optimal parameters.

The contribution of this work is implementation, evaluation and demonstration of Whisper-Streaming. Given that Whisper-Streaming can be quickly and easily packaged into a product, we want to ensure that the most recent scientific results, such as the algorithm for simultaneous mode, can be accessible to and be used by industrial researchers and engineers. Furthermore, we want to reliably evaluate the performance of our implementation and share the results with the research community, to further drive research and development of real-time transcription solutions which have real-life use cases. We expect that our results can be used as strong baselines for future comparison.

We make Whisper-Streaming publicly available[1] along with a demonstration video.[2]

2 Background

In this section, we describe the background for the back-end components of our work.

[1]https://github.com/ufal/whisper_streaming
[2]https://vimeo.com/840442741

Proceedings of the 13th International Joint Conference on Natural Language Processing and the 3rd Conference of the Asia-Pacific Chapter of the Association for Computational Linguistics: System Demonstrations, pages 17–24
November 1–4, 2023.

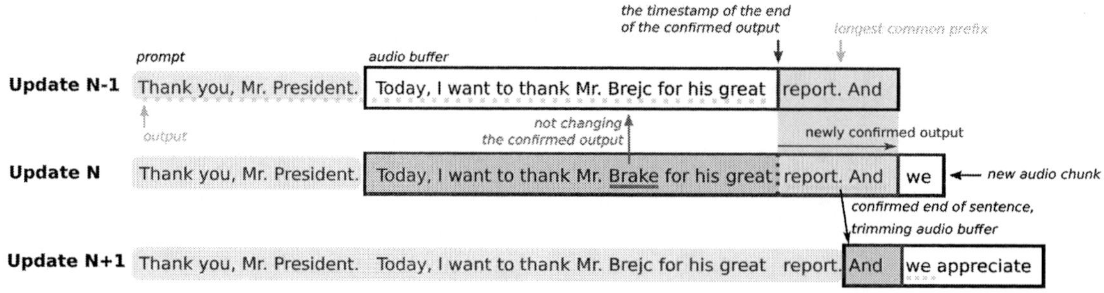

Figure 1: Illustration of processing three consecutive updates. The yellow highlighted text is a "prompt", the previous context to follow. The black-bordered rectangle is an audio buffer, and the text inside is Whisper's transcript generated from that sound segment. The blue vertical line is a timestamp that splits the buffer to two parts, the left being previously confirmed, and the right one is unconfirmed. The LocalAgreement-2 policy, or searching the longest common prefix, is applied on the unconfirmed (right) part in two subsequent updates. The longest common prefix is highlighted in green and the green underline highlights the *newly* confirmed output, whereas the green dashed underline indicates previously and subsequently confirmed output. The gray underline demonstrates an update in the confirmed part that is disregarded.

Whisper (Radford et al., 2022) is a Transformer model for speech-to-text transcription and translation trained on a massive amount of multilingual data. We use "large-v2"[3] model because it achieves the highest quality of all Whisper model size options. Since the original release of the whisper backend is rather slow, we use the `faster-whisper`[4] reimplementation of Whisper inference using CTranslate2, a fast inference engine for Transformer models. It is approximately four times faster than the standard implementation (as reported by the authors). We use it with 16-bit float precision.

Although we primarily use Whisper, the underlying model in our implementation can be easily replaced by any other speech-to-text transcription or translation model (e.g. MMS, Pratap et al., 2023) if it produces word-level timestamps and punctuation.

Streaming Let us assume a model M that processes a source sequence $c_1, \cdots, c_n$ into a target sequence $t_1, \cdots, t_m$, given a previous target s that can be used for for inter-sentence coherence. Streaming involves receiving the source sequence consecutively, one chunk at a time, and producing the target simultaneously. A *streaming policy* P predicts a target segment t_T at time T as $t_T := P_M(c_{i<T}|s, t_{j<T})$. It operates the model M on available source chunks $c_{i<T}$, previous sequence target s, and previous target segments $t_{j<T}$. The policy is triggered every time a new source segment is available. An empty target segment can be emitted, e.g. when waiting for context. The policy aims to minimize latency and maximize target quality.

Streaming was originally proposed for simultaneous translation (Ma et al., 2019), but it is applicable for any sequence-to-sequence task including ASR. Dong et al. (2022) give a summary of streaming speech translation.

LocalAgreement (Liu et al., 2020) is a streaming policy that outputs the longest common prefix of the model on n consecutive source chunks, or an empty segment when less than n chunks are available. Based on the IWSLT 2022 shared task on simultaneous translation, the CUNI-KIT system compared LocalAgreement to other policies (hold-n and wait-k) with different chunk sizes. They found that LocalAgreement with $n = 2$ was the most effective policy. Therefore, we use LocalAgreement-2 for identifying stabilized target segments.

3 Whisper-Streaming

We describe the core components and inner workings of Whisper-Streaming. It consists of the update loop, audio buffer, skipping the confirmed output in audio buffer, trimming the buffer, joining for inter-sentence context, and optional voice activity detection.

Update Loop The main part of Whisper-Streaming is a program that utilizes a loop to receive source audio chunks and trigger streaming

[3] `https://huggingface.co/openai/whisper-large-v2`

[4] `https://github.com/guillaumekln/faster-whisper`

policy updates. The parameter MinChunkSize controls the latency and quality, and determines the minimal duration processed per iteration. If the update computation exceeds MinChunkSize, the next update is performed immediately on the accumulated audio input. This parameter impacts both latency and quality.

Audio buffer Whisper is trained to handle sequences that are up to 30 seconds long and contain one full sentence. It provides punctuation and word-level timestamps.[5] The process is illustrated in Figure 1. Each update involves storing incoming audio at the top of the audio buffer and processing the entire buffer with Whisper. We keep an invariant that the buffer always starts with a new sentence, to maintain the high quality of Whisper. LocalAgreement-2 is applied to the current and previous Whisper output. The timestamp of the last word in the "confirmed output" is saved. In subsequent updates, we always reprocess Whisper from the beginning of the buffer, including the portion preceding the last "confirmed output" timestamp (indicated by the gray background in Figure 1). Changes to the transcription in the confirmed portion are disregarded, as they are often insignificant in terms of meaning alteration.

Skipping the confirmed part When determining the position of transcribed words relative to the last confirmed word from the previous update, we account for the potential inaccuracies and updates in Whisper timestamps due to new audio chunks. If a word's timestamp falls within a 1-second interval from the last confirmed word, we compare its preceding n-grams (where n ranges from 1 to 5) with the suffix in the last confirmed output. If they match, we skip those words. However, this rule can be further enhanced in future work by incorporating measures such as setting and fine-tuning a character edit distance threshold, trimming punctuation and casing from the n-grams, etc.

Trimming the audio buffer To avoid inacceptably long spikes in latenc, the audio buffer is limited to around 30 seconds. When the confirmed output includes a sentence-ending punctuation mark followed by a word starting a new sentence, the buffer is trimmed at the punctuation mark's timestamp. A language specific sentence segmentation tool (e.g. Koehn et al., 2007) is used for this purpose, ensuring that the buffer always contains a single sentence. Despite this, if the buffer length exceeds 30 seconds, we retain the last confirmed segment marked by Whisper.

Joining for inter-sentence context The Whisper transcribe function utilizes a "prompt" parameter to maintain consistency within a document (consistent style, terminology, and inter-sentence references). We extract the last 200 words from the confirmed output of previous audio buffers as the "prompt" parameter, as shown in Figure 1 (yellow backgrounded text).

Voice activity detection There is a parameter to activate or deactivate Whisper's default voice activity detection (VAD) filter, impacting both quality and latency.

4 Benchmarking Settings

We describe the dataset for evaluation, metrics, settings and hardware we used to evaluate our model.

Evaluation Data For latency and quality analysis, we utilize the dev set of the manually transcribed ESIC corpus (Macháček et al., 2021) for English, German, and Czech ASR containing 179 documents. This corpus contains 5 hours of original English speeches from the European Parliament, including simultaneous interpreting into German and Czech. It provides audio tracks with manual transcripts and word-level timestamps.

WER We use word error rate (WER) after removing punctuation and casing as the standard measure of ASR quality.

Latency In our latency analysis, we implement our own method wherein we use the timestamps provided in the ESIC corpus to align the gold transcripts to the ASR output using edit distance.[6] This allows us to determine the edit operations for each gold word. We calculate the ASR latency by measuring the time difference between when the ASR emitted a word and when the corresponding gold word was spoken, excluding words deleted by the ASR. We compute the average latency within each document and, when comparing different setups across multiple documents, we report the average latency along with standard deviation.

[5] When using "faster-whisper" or aannother implementation that supports it.

[6] https://pypi.org/project/edlib/

GPU	VAD	% WER	latency [s]
A40	**off**	**5.8±0.9**	**2.85±0.45**
A40	on	5.2±0.9	3.12±0.36
L40	off	5.1±1.0	3.58±0.62
L40	on	5.0±0.6	3.96±0.81

Table 1: Average (±stddev) WER and latency of English ASR of 10 repeated runs of ESIC dev.20080925.013_007 document, with MinChunkSize 0.1 seconds, using or not using VAD filter, on two GPU types. Bold is the setup that we later use.

Hardware For benchmarking, we use NVIDIA A40 GPUs. We run Whisper on a computer in a cluster that is used by other processes at the same time, which may allocate the same resources and influence the latency. Since it is not always possible to have a dedicated server for a given service, this makes our evaluation very realistic. Since there will be variations in the latency metrics, we report mean and standard deviations.

Ensuring Reproducibility We simulate real-time processing of long-form transcription and record the times when Whisper emitted the outputs. We run the simulation on computers in a cluster that are not entirely under our control. For our simulation process, we block one GPU and a sufficient number of CPUs and RAM capacity. However, it can happen that other processes run at the same time, making a CPU and RAM load that is unpredictably slowing down our simulation. If the MinChunkSize is smaller than time for processing an update, then two runs of the same simulation have different segmentation to chunks, leading to different WER and latency.

Therefore, we run simulation of the same setup of one document 10 times, to measure the standard deviation of the latency and quality. The setup is English transcription of the ESIC dev.20080925.013_007 document that is 3 minutes 36 seconds long, on NVIDIA A40 or L40 GPU with 48GB GPU RAM, 8 blocked CPU cores and 200GB of CPU RAM, with or without VAD filter, with MinChunkSize 0.1 seconds.

The results are in Table 1. We observe small, negligible standard deviation in WER, below or near 1%. The standard deviation in the average latency is much larger, from 0.36 to 0.81 seconds depending on the setup. We conclude that we must be aware of the standard deviation of latency due to uncontrollable computation conditions.

5 Results

We evaluated Whisper-Streaming with various setups for English, German and Czech ASR. We first show the impact of outliers and voice activity detection (VAD) to determine optimal settings, and then present our main results with these settings.

Outliers After processing many setups, we observed extraordinarily high WER on English ASR of a document dev2.20101213.015_018_EN_Gallagher. We realized it is due to noise in the ESIC data set. The first half of the mentioned document is in Irish, and not English as intended. Only the English part is transcribed in gold, but Whisper transcribed both, leading to more precise transcription than the reference. Except of the Gallagher document, all the reported setups achieved WER between 0 and 52%, and average latency between 0 and 16.1 seconds.

VAD We studied the effect of VAD (voice activity detection) filter that is integrated within Whisper backend. The results are in Table 2 and Figure 2. We realized that in ESIC corpus, it is advisable to deactivate the VAD filter for the English original speech, because it is very fluent, not interleaved with silence and has no non-voice sounds. Without VAD, the quality remains nearly the same (difference within 0.2% WER), and the average latency was substantially lower, between 0.23 to 0.41 seconds.

For the processing of simultaneous interpreting, we recommend activating the VAD filter. The speech of a simultaneous interpreter contains many pauses, especially when waiting for context. With VAD, the latency was only 0.1 seconds larger, because VAD often filters out silence, which reduces the processing load. The quality with VAD was substantially higher, by 2 to 3 % WER with shorter MinChunkSize on German. With large chunk sizes, the quality is nearly the same (0.3 % WER difference with 2 seconds MinChunkSize) because a large chunk size causes the model to have large context and thus a low chance for risking uncertain output. Therefore, we activated VAD for German and Czech simultaneous interpreting, and we deactivated it for English original speech.

For a real-life setup, we recommend starting Whisper-Streaming shortly before the speech actually starts, so that the first words are not missed, along with turning the VAD filter on so that the

	m.ch.	avg. % WER off	on	diff	avg. latency [s] off	on	diff
en	0.1s	8.4	8.3	-0.1	**3.30**	3.72	+0.41
	0.5s	8.5	8.3	-0.2	**3.27**	3.54	+0.27
	1.0s	8.1	8.1	+0.1	**3.62**	3.88	+0.26
	2.0s	8.0	7.9	-0.0	**5.45**	5.68	+0.23
de	0.1s	12.8	**9.7**	-3.1	3.83	3.93	+0.10
	0.5s	12.3	**9.5**	-2.8	3.97	4.11	+0.14
	1.0s	11.4	**9.4**	-2.0	4.19	4.37	+0.18
	2.0s	9.6	**9.3**	-0.3	5.79	5.94	+0.15

Table 2: Impact of VAD filter on WER and latency on ESIC dev on the streaming ASR with different minimum chunk size (m.ch., in seconds) of the English original speech (en) and German simultaneous interpreting (de). We highlight the remarkable benefit in bold: the original speech without pauses is processed with lower latency (by 0.23 seconds or more) and comparable quality with VAD off. On the contrary, the VAD on achieves higher quality for interpreting with frequent pauses, with small difference in latency.

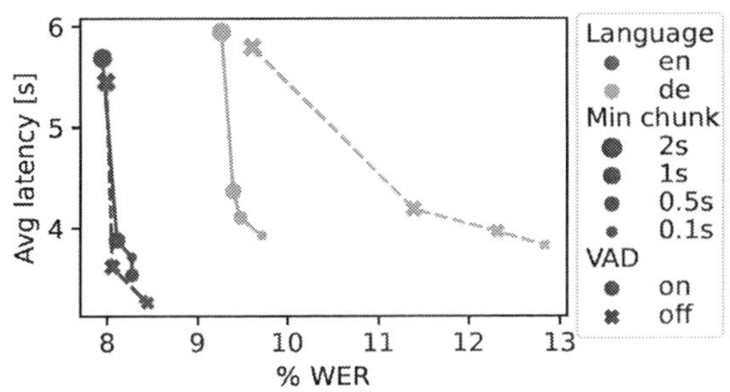

Figure 2: Impact of VAD filter on latency and quality. The striking difference in VAD activated or deactivated for English vs German is due to German being the speech of an interpreter.

silence and non-voice sounds do not cause Whisper to make mistakes. If reducing the latency is important, an adaptive protocol for setting VAD on and off can be implemented.

Performance Table 3 and Figure 3 summarize the WER and average latency of Whisper-Streaming on ESIC validation set for the three language tracks. Overall, with 1 second MinChunkSize, the average latency is 3.3 seconds for English, 4.4 seconds for German and 4.8 seconds for Czech, while the WER is by 2% higher than in the offline mode for English and German, and by 6% higher for Czech. Both WER and latency is the lowest on English, followed by German and Czech. This is related to the amount of language specific data used for training Whisper, as well as the morphological complexity of these languages. The latency increases with larger uncertainty because it requires more updates for an agreement. Moreover, the larger MinChunkSize, the larger the latency, but higher the quality because the system has sufficient context.

Offline mode WER We contrast the results with setups that serve as maximum performance estimates. One of them is offline mode in which processing of the whole audio document is done after recording, without any limitations on processing time. It is the default and most optimized setup for Whisper. The WER in offline mode and with VAD is lower than in streaming mode because the context size is not restricted. The model can use even the right (future) context that is unavailable or limited in streaming mode. Moreover, the internal segmentation of the long-form speech into processing chunks is optimized in the offline mode.

Computationally unaware latency Another contrastive setup is computationally unaware simulation. It uses an unrealistic assumption that computation for Whisper processing any audio segment is instant, so that the latency caused by computation is not included in the latency measurement. The measurement includes latency caused by uncertainty in the language. The gap between latency in computationally unaware and aware evaluation can be reduced by optimizing the hardware or inference algorithm. Computationally unaware latency can be reduced by improving the model or streaming policy.

We observe that the average computationally unaware latency is approximately twice the chunk size. This is expected because we use local agreement of two consecutive updates. However, the processing of English is actually faster, little less than twice the chunk size. We hypothesize that this could be caused by the anticipation ability of Whisper model. The second possible reason is the inaccuracy of the gold timestamps in ESIC. The timestamps were computed by automatic forced alignment, and thus they may be less accurate in non-standard situations such as overlapping and non-transcribed speech, e.g. hesitations and foreign language insertions.

6 System Demonstration

Demonstration video is available at `https://vimeo.com/840442741`. It is a screencast video of Whisper-Streaming real-time outputs that pro-

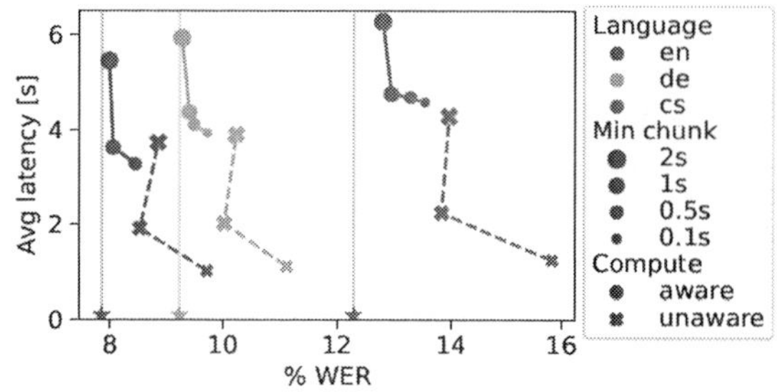

Figure 3: Latency and quality in computationally aware and unaware simulations (solid lines and dots vs dashed lines and crosses), together with offline WER (stars and light vertical lines). VAD is deactivated for English, and activated for the other two.

lang.	% WER offline	m.ch.	% WER un.	% WER aw.	latency [s] un.	latency [s] aw.	latency [s] diff
en	7.9	0.5s	9.7	8.5	1.02	3.27	+2.25
		1.0s	8.5	8.1	1.91	3.62	+1.71
		2.0s	8.8	8.0	3.73	5.45	+1.73
de	9.2	0.5s	11.1	9.5	1.11	4.11	+3.00
		1.0s	10.0	9.4	2.02	4.37	+2.35
		2.0s	10.2	9.3	3.89	5.94	+2.05
cs	12.3	0.5s	15.8	13.3	1.25	4.69	+3.44
		1.0s	13.8	12.9	2.24	4.76	+2.51
		2.0s	14.0	12.8	4.29	6.29	+2.00

Table 3: WER and average latency of Whisper-Streaming on ESIC dev set in three language tracks using different MinChunkSize ("m.ch."). The realistic setup is computationally aware ("aw."), put into contrast with offline WER ("offline") and with the computationally unaware simulation ("un."). The data are the same as in Figure 3.

cesses live ASR on one ESIC document in three parallel instances for English, German and Czech speech, the original and simultaneous interpreting. The video shows a contrast to gold transcripts with original timing, so that the latency can be observed. The video also contains color highlighting for ASR errors.

Integration with ELITR To demonstrate practical usability, we integrate Whisper-Streaming with the ELITR (European Live Translator, Bojar et al., 2020) framework for complex distributed systems for multi-source and multi-target live speech transcription and translation (Bojar et al., 2021a). Within Whisper-Streaming, we implement and release a server that is connected as a worker to Mediator server (Franceschini et al., 2020). Mediator allows a client to request a service of a worker. The client is then allowed to further process the text outputs received by the worker, e.g. translate them with another worker and present them at the web view server that delivers real-time captions to event participants during a live multilingual event.

Evaluation event We evaluated Whisper-Streaming as a component in an experimental live speech translation service at a multilingual conference. For this, we built a pipeline that used five parallel Whisper-Streaming workers, three of them for ASR only (English, Czech and Ukrainian), and two for speech translation (Czech-to-English and Ukrainian-to-English). There were three parallel language streams at the conference, Czech, English and Ukrainian. One of the languages was spoken at the main floor, and the others were provided by human simultaneous interpreting.

A human operator (as in Bojar et al., 2021b) was controlling the technical setup and the outputs using the language knowledge and had an option to redirect the streams, if necessary. The qualitative evaluation at the event showed that Whisper-Streaming is a robust and reliable part of the service, reaching acceptable latency and unexpectedly high quality on English, Czech and Ukrainian long-form speech.

Demonstration at AACL Our system demonstration at the IJCNLP-AACL 2023 conference will use the ELITR framework. We will either simulate speech source from a recording, or allow participants to speak into microphone in any of the 97 languages supported by Whisper, and observe the real-time outputs.

7 Conclusion

We implemented, evaluated and demonstrated Whisper-Streaming, a tool that effectively operates an offline ASR model Whisper, with 3.3 second average computationally aware latency on English ESIC corpus. We described and explained the implementation and its underlying components, including LocalAgreement algorithm for streaming. Lastly, we demonstrated the robustness and practical usability at a real-life multi-lingual conference.

8 Limitations

The data collected in ESIC corpus were created relatively long time ago. It raises concerns about potential leakage into Whisper training set, which could compromise our evaluation. Additionally, performance tests on more affordable hardware are pending, highlighting the need for further evaluation in terms of computational cost.

It is worth noting that the reported latency and quality metrics obtained from ESIC may not be fully generalizable to other languages or language variants due to the nature of the corpus.

Furthermore, our focus is on demonstrating the online capabilities of Whisper rather than optimizing the algorithm or implementation. It is important to recognize that the actual latency experienced may fluctuate, and the reported average latency serves as an indicative measure without providing an upper bound. The streaming policy would need certain modifications to guarantee a maximum latency, at a possible loss in quality.

Lastly, we have not conducted comparison tests to other state-of-the-art systems, e.g. from IWSLT, because a common evaluation framework is pending, as well as X-to-English long-form speech test set.

Acknowledgements

This research was partially supported by the grants 19-26934X (NEUREM3) of the Czech Science Foundation, and SVV project number 260 698.

References

Ondřej Bojar, Dominik Macháček, Sangeet Sagar, Otakar Smrž, Jonáš Kratochvíl, Ebrahim Ansari, Dario Franceschini, Chiara Canton, Ivan Simonini, Thai-Son Nguyen, Felix Schneider, Sebastian Stücker, Alex Waibel, Barry Haddow, Rico Sennrich, and Philip Williams. 2020. ELITR: European live translator. In *Proceedings of the 22nd Annual Conference of the European Association for Machine Translation*, pages 463–464, Lisboa, Portugal. European Association for Machine Translation.

Ondřej Bojar, Dominik Macháček, Sangeet Sagar, Otakar Smrž, Jonáš Kratochvíl, Peter Polák, Ebrahim Ansari, Mohammad Mahmoudi, Rishu Kumar, Dario Franceschini, Chiara Canton, Ivan Simonini, Thai-Son Nguyen, Felix Schneider, Sebastian Stüker, Alex Waibel, Barry Haddow, Rico Sennrich, and Philip Williams. 2021a. ELITR multilingual live subtitling: Demo and strategy. In *Proceedings of the 16th Conference of the European Chapter of the Association for Computational Linguistics: System Demonstrations*, pages 271–277, Online. Association for Computational Linguistics.

Ondřej Bojar, Vojtěch Srdečný, Rishu Kumar, Otakar Smrž, Felix Schneider, Barry Haddow, Phil Williams, and Chiara Canton. 2021b. Operating a complex SLT system with speakers and human interpreters. In *Proceedings of the 1st Workshop on Automatic Spoken Language Translation in Real-World Settings (ASLTRW)*, pages 23–34, Virtual. Association for Machine Translation in the Americas.

Qian Dong, Yaoming Zhu, Mingxuan Wang, and Lei Li. 2022. Learning when to translate for streaming speech. In *Proceedings of the 60th Annual Meeting of the Association for Computational Linguistics (Volume 1: Long Papers)*, pages 680–694, Dublin, Ireland. Association for Computational Linguistics.

Dario Franceschini, Chiara Canton, Ivan Simonini, Armin Schweinfurth, Adelheid Glott, Sebastian Stüker, Thai-Son Nguyen, Felix Schneider, Thanh-Le Ha, Alex Waibel, Barry Haddow, Philip Williams, Rico Sennrich, Ondřej Bojar, Sangeet Sagar, Dominik Macháček, and Otakar Smrž. 2020. Removing European language barriers with innovative machine translation technology. In *Proceedings of the 1st International Workshop on Language Technology Platforms*, pages 44–49, Marseille, France. European Language Resources Association.

Philipp Koehn, Hieu Hoang, Alexandra Birch, Chris Callison-Burch, Marcello Federico, Nicola Bertoldi, Brooke Cowan, Wade Shen, Christine Moran, Richard Zens, Chris Dyer, Ondřej Bojar, Alexandra Constantin, and Evan Herbst. 2007. Moses: Open source toolkit for statistical machine translation. In *Proceedings of the 45th Annual Meeting of the Association for Computational Linguistics Companion Volume Proceedings of the Demo and Poster Sessions*, pages 177–180, Prague, Czech Republic. Association for Computational Linguistics.

Danni Liu, Gerasimos Spanakis, and Jan Niehues. 2020. Low-Latency Sequence-to-Sequence Speech Recognition and Translation by Partial Hypothesis Selection. In *Proc. Interspeech 2020*, pages 3620–3624.

Mingbo Ma, Liang Huang, Hao Xiong, Renjie Zheng, Kaibo Liu, Baigong Zheng, Chuanqiang Zhang, Zhongjun He, Hairong Liu, Xing Li, Hua Wu, and Haifeng Wang. 2019. STACL: Simultaneous translation with implicit anticipation and controllable latency using prefix-to-prefix framework. In *Proceedings of the 57th Annual Meeting of the Association for Computational Linguistics*, pages 3025–3036, Florence, Italy. Association for Computational Linguistics.

Dominik Macháček, Matúš Žilinec, and Ondřej Bojar. 2021. Lost in Interpreting: Speech Translation from Source or Interpreter? In *Proc. Interspeech 2021*, pages 2376–2380.

Peter Polák, Ngoc-Quan Pham, Tuan Nam Nguyen, Danni Liu, Carlos Mullov, Jan Niehues, Ondřej Bojar, and Alexander Waibel. 2022. CUNI-KIT system for simultaneous speech translation task at IWSLT 2022. In *Proceedings of the 19th International Conference on Spoken Language Translation (IWSLT 2022)*, pages 277–285, Dublin, Ireland (in-person and online). Association for Computational Linguistics.

Vineel Pratap, Andros Tjandra, Bowen Shi, Paden Tomasello, Arun Babu, Sayani Kundu, Ali Elkahky, Zhaoheng Ni, Apoorv Vyas, Maryam Fazel-Zarandi, Alexei Baevski, Yossi Adi, Xiaohui Zhang, Wei-Ning Hsu, Alexis Conneau, and Michael Auli. 2023. Scaling speech technology to 1,000+ languages. *arXiv*.

Alec Radford, Jong Wook Kim, Tao Xu, Greg Brockman, Christine McLeavey, and Ilya Sutskever. 2022. Robust speech recognition via large-scale weak supervision.

LambdaKG: A Library for Pre-trained Language Model-Based Knowledge Graph Embeddings

Xin Xie[1]*, **Zhoubo Li**[1]*, **Xiaohan Wang**[1]*, **Zekun Xi**[1], **Ningyu Zhang**[1]†
[1] Zhejiang University
{xx2020,zhoubo.li,wangxh07,zhangningyu}@zju.edu.cn,
https://zjunlp.github.io/project/promptkg/

Abstract

Knowledge Graphs (KGs) often have two characteristics: heterogeneous graph structure and text-rich entity/relation information. Text-based KG embeddings can represent entities by encoding descriptions with pre-trained language models, but no open-sourced library is specifically designed for KGs with PLMs at present. In this paper, we present **LambdaKG**, a library for KGE that equips with many pre-trained language models (e.g., BERT, BART, T5, GPT-3) and supports various tasks (e.g., knowledge graph completion, question answering, recommendation, and knowledge probing). **LambdaKG** is publicly open-sourced[1], with a demo video[2] and long-term maintenance.

1 Introduction

Knowledge Graphs (KGs) encode real-world facts as structured data and have drawn significant attention from academia, and industry (Zhang et al., 2022b). Knowledge Graph Embedding (KGE) aims to project the relations and entities into a continuous vector space, which can enhance knowledge reasoning abilities and feasibly be applied to downstream tasks: question answering (Saxena et al., 2022), recommendation (Zhang et al., 2021) and so on (Chen et al., 2022b). Previous **embedding-based** KGE methods, such as TransE (Bordes et al., 2013), involved embedding relational knowledge into a vector space and subsequently optimizing the target object by applying a pre-defined scoring function to those vectors. A few remarkable embedding-based KGE toolkits have been developed, such as OpenKE (Han et al., 2018), LibKGE (Broscheit et al., 2020), PyKEEN (Ali et al., 2021), CogKGE (Jin et al., 2022) and NeuralKG (Zhang et al., 2022c). Nevertheless, these embedding-based KGE approaches are restricted in expressiveness regarding the shallow network architectures without using any side information (e.g., textual description).

By comparison with embedding-based KGE approaches, text-based methods incorporate available texts for KGE. With the development of Pre-trained Language Models (PLMs), many text-based models (Xie et al., 2022; Saxena et al., 2022; Kim et al., 2020; Markowitz et al., 2022; Chen et al., 2022a; Liu et al., 2022) have been proposed, which can obtain promising performance and take advantage of allocating a fixed memory footprint for large-scale real-world KGs. Recently, large language models (LLMs) (e.g., GPT-3 (Brown et al., 2020), ChatGPT (OpenAI, 2022)) further demonstrated the ability to perform a variety of natural language processing (NLP) tasks without adaptation, providing potential opportunities of better knowledge representations. However, there is **no comprehensive open-sourced library particularly designed for KGE with PLMs at present**, which makes it challenging to test new methods and make rigorous comparisons with previous approaches.

In this paper, we share with the community a pre-trained **LA**nguage **M**odel-**B**ase**D** libr**A**ry for **KG**Es and applications called **LambdaKG** (MIT License), which supports various cutting-edge models. Specifically, we equip **LambdaKG** with both small PLMs, e.g., BERT (Devlin et al., 2018; Yao et al., 2019), BART (Lewis et al., 2020; Liu et al., 2021), T5 (Raffel et al., 2020; Saxena et al., 2022); and large PLMs, e.g., GPT-3 (Brown et al., 2020), ChatGPT (OpenAI, 2022), by developing two major paradigms of discrimination-based and generation-based methods for KGEs. **LambdaKG** supports factual and commonsense KGs with diverse tasks, including KG completion, question answering, recommendation, and knowledge probing (LAMA). We will provide maintenance to meet new tasks, new requests and fix bugs.

* Equal contribution and shared co-first authorship.
† Corresponding author.
[1]Code: https://github.com/zjunlp/PromptKG/tree/main/lambdaKG
[2]Video: http://deepke.zjukg.cn/lambdakg.mp4

Proceedings of the 13th International Joint Conference on Natural Language Processing and the 3rd Conference of the Asia-Pacific Chapter of the Association for Computational Linguistics: System Demonstrations, pages 25–33
November 1–4, 2023.

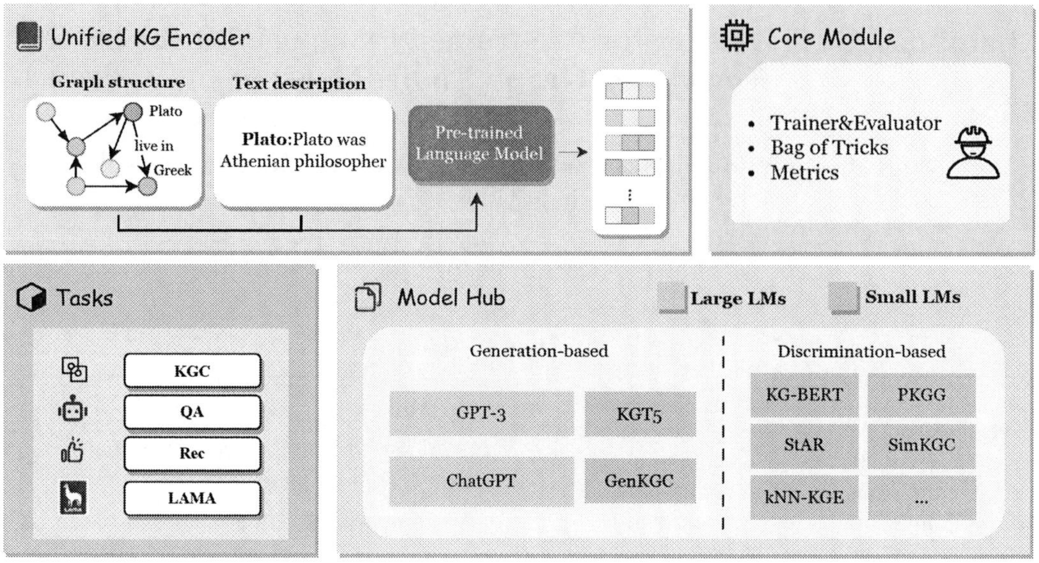

Figure 1: The architecture and features of **LambdaKG**.

2 System Architecture

The overall features & architecture of **LambdaKG** are presented in Figure 1. We will detail two major types of PLM-based KGE methods (discrimination-based and generation-based) with various PLMs.

Our design principles are: 1) *Core Module with Unified KG Encoder*: **LambdaKG** utilizes a unified encoder to pack graph structure and text semantics, with convenient `Trainer&Evaluator`, `Metric`, and `Bag of Tricks`; 2) *Model Hub*: **LambdaKG** is integrated with many cutting-edge PLM-based KGE models; 3) *Flexible Downstream Tasks*: **LambdaKG** disentangles KG representation learning and downstream tasks.

2.1 Core Module

2.1.1 Trainer&Evaluator

Typically, the training process with **LambdaKG** can be decomposed into several distinct steps, such as the forward and backward passes (i.e., `training_step`), logging of intermediate results (`log`), and model evaluation (`evaluate_step`). Our `Trainer` class provides a flexible and modular framework for training different types of models, with customizable functions to handle various tasks, such as computing the loss function and updating model parameters. Moreover, the `Trainer` class allows users to define their own plugins, which can be integrated seamlessly into the training pipeline to provide additional functionalities.

2.1.2 Metric

We design the `Metric` class to evaluate different models for various tasks. Specifically, we use `hits@k` with `k` values of 1, 3, 10 and *mean rank (MR)* as the evaluation metrics. Hits@k measures the proportion of correct predictions among the top k-ranked results, while MR calculates the average rank of the correct answer. We also implement `BLEU-1` score to evaluate the commonsense KG completion tasks following Hwang et al. (2021).

2.1.3 Bag of Tricks

All models in the **LambdaKG** are based on PLMs, and we equip a bag of tricks of training techniques to improve their performance. In particular, we employ different pluggable modules such as `label smoothing` and `exponential moving average` to assist in the training of models. We implement `early stopping` and `fast run` modules to prevent overfitting with small data by introducing early stopping and automatic verification mechanisms. Furthermore, we integrate an off-the-shelf `Top-k negative sampling strategy` to enhance the training by selecting the most informative negative samples during the training process.

2.2 Unified KG Encoder

Since **LambdaKG** is based on PLMs, the most critical thing is to convert structural triples into plain natural language for PLMs to understand. We introduce a unified KG encoder to represent graph structure and text semantics, supporting different

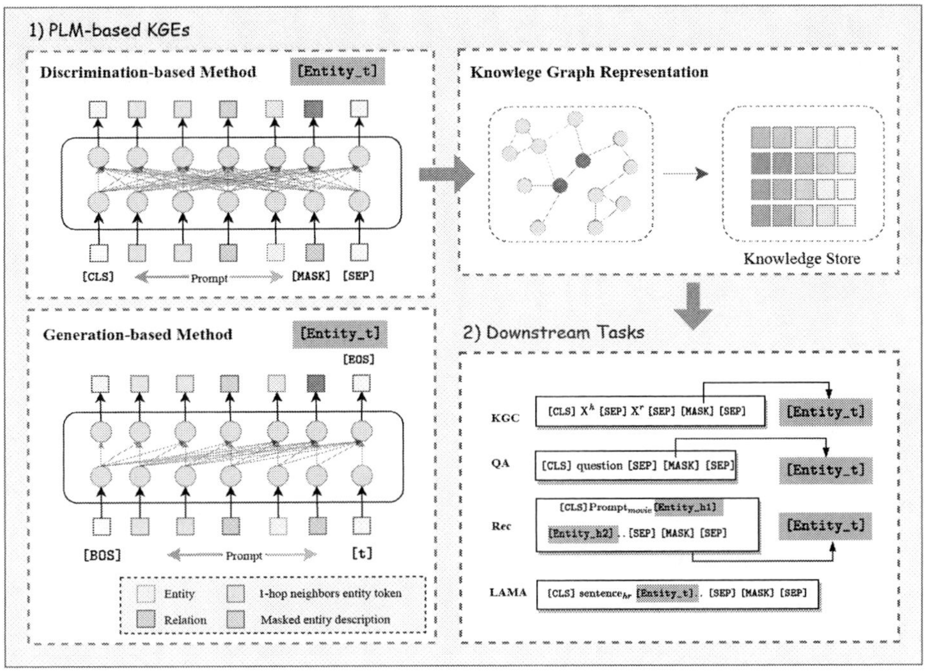

Figure 2: PLM-based KGEs in **LambdaKG** and those KGEs can be applied to KGC, QA, recommendation and knowledge probing. *Entity_t* refers to the target tail entity, answer entity, recommended items, and target tail entity for different tasks, which follows the pre-train (obtain the embedding) and fine-tune paradigm (task-specific tuning).

types of PLM-based KGE methods. To encode the graph structure, we sample 1-hop neighbor entities and concatenate their tokens as input for implicit structure information. With such a unified KG encoder, **LambdaKG** can encode both heterogeneous graph structure and text-rich semantic information. For the discrimination-based method, the input is built on the plain text description:

$$X_{\text{hr pair}} = \texttt{[CLS]}\ X^h \texttt{[SEP]}\ X^r\ \texttt{[SEP]} \\ X_{\text{tail}} = \texttt{[CLS]}\ X^t\ \texttt{[SEP]}. \quad (1)$$

where X^h, X^r, and X^t refer to the text sequence of the head entity, relation, and tail entity, respectively. Referring to some prompt learning methods like kNN-KGE (Zhang et al., 2022a), we represent entities and relations in KG with special tokens (See §2.3) and obtain the input as:

$$X = \texttt{[CLS]} X^h \texttt{[Entity h] [SEP]}\ X^r\ \texttt{[SEP] [MASK] [SEP]}, \quad (2)$$

where `[Entity h]` represents the special token to the head entity.

For the generation-based model, we leverage the tokens in X^h and X^r to optimize the model with the label X^t. When predicting the head entity, we add a special token `[reverse]` in the input sequence for reverse reasoning.

2.3 Model Hub

As shown in Figure 2 and Table 1, **LambdaKG** consists of a `Model Hub` which supports many representative PLM-based KGE methods, mainly follow the two major paradigms of discrimination-based methods and generation-based methods as:

Discrimination-based methods There are three kinds of models based on the discrimination method: the first one (e.g., KG-BERT (Yao et al., 2019), PKGC (Lv et al., 2022)) utilizes a single encoder to encode triples of KG with text description; another kind of model (e.g., StAR (Wang et al., 2021), SimKGC (Wang et al., 2022)) leverages siamese encoder (two-tower models) with PLMs to encode entities and relations respectively. For the first kind, the score of each triple is expressed as:

$$\text{Score}(h, r, t) = \text{TransformerEnc}(X^h, X^r, X^t), \quad (3)$$

where TransformerEnc is the BERT model followed by a binary classifier. However, these models have to iterate all the entities calculating scores to decide the correct one, which is computation-intensive, as shown in Table 1. In contrast, two-tower models like StAR (Wang et al., 2021) and SimKGC (Wang et al., 2022) usually encode $\langle h, r\rangle$ and t to obtain the embeddings. Then, they use a

Model	PLM	Support Tasks	Complexity
KGBERT (Yao et al., 2019)	MLM	KGC	$\mathcal{O}(\|L\|^2\|\mathcal{E}\|^2\|\mathcal{R}\|)$
StAR (Wang et al., 2021)	MLM	KGC	$\mathcal{O}(\|L/2\|^2\|\mathcal{E}\|(1+\|\mathcal{R}\|))$
SimKGC (Wang et al., 2022)	MLM	KGC	$\mathcal{O}(\|L/2\|^2\|\mathcal{E}\|(1+\|\mathcal{R}\|))$
kNN-KGE (Zhang et al., 2022a)	MLM	KGC, LAMA	$\mathcal{O}(\|L\|^2\|\mathcal{E}\|\|\mathcal{R}\|)$
KGT5 (Saxena et al., 2022)	Seq2Seq	KGC, QA	$\mathcal{O}(\|L/2\|^3\|\mathcal{E}\|\|\mathcal{R}\|)$
GenKGC (Xie et al., 2022)	Seq2Seq	KGC, QA	$\mathcal{O}(\|L/2\|^3\|\mathcal{E}\|\|\mathcal{R}\|)$

Table 1: Comparison of different methods based on small PLMs. $|L|$ is the length of the triple description. $|L/2|$ can be seen as the length of entity tokens. $|\mathcal{E}|$ and $|\mathcal{R}|$ are the numbers of all unique entities and relations in the graph respectively.

score function to predict the correct tail entity from the candidates, denoted by:

$$\text{Score}(\langle h, r\rangle, t) = \cos(e_{\langle h,r\rangle}, e_t). \tag{4}$$

The final kind of model, e.g., kNN-KGE (Zhang et al., 2022a), utilizes masked language modeling for KGE, which shares the same architecture as normal discrimination PLMs. Note that there are two modules in the normal PLMs: a *word embedding layer* to embed the token ids into semantic space and an *encoder* to generate context-aware token embedding. Here, we take the masked language model and **treat entities and relations as special tokens** in the "word embedding layer". As shown in Figure 2, the model predicts the correct tail entity with the sequence of the head entity and relation token and their descriptions. For the entity/relation embedding, we freeze the *encoder layer*, only tuning the *entity embedding layer*, to optimize the loss function:

$$\mathcal{L} = -\frac{1}{|\mathcal{E}|}\sum_{e_j \in \mathcal{E}} \mathbb{I}(e_j = e_i) \log p\left(\texttt{[MASK]} = e_j \mid X^i; \Theta\right), \tag{5}$$

where Θ represents the parameters of the model, X^i and e_i is the description and the embedding of entity i.

Generation-based methods Generation-based models formulate KG completion or other KG-intensive tasks as sequence-to-sequence generation. Given a triple with the tail entity missing $(h, r, ?)$, models are fed with $\langle X^h, X^r\rangle$ and then output X^t. In the training procedure, generative models maximize the conditional probability:

$$\text{Score}(h, r, t) = \prod_{i=1}^{|X^t|} p(x_i^t | x_1^t, x_2^t, ..., x_{i-1}^t; \langle X^h, X^r\rangle). \tag{6}$$

To guarantee the consistency of decoding sequential schemas and tokens in KG, GenKGC (Xie et al., 2022) proposes an entity-aware hierarchical decoder to constrain X^t. Besides, KGT5 (Saxena et al., 2022) proposes to pre-train generation-based PLMs with text descriptions for KG representation.

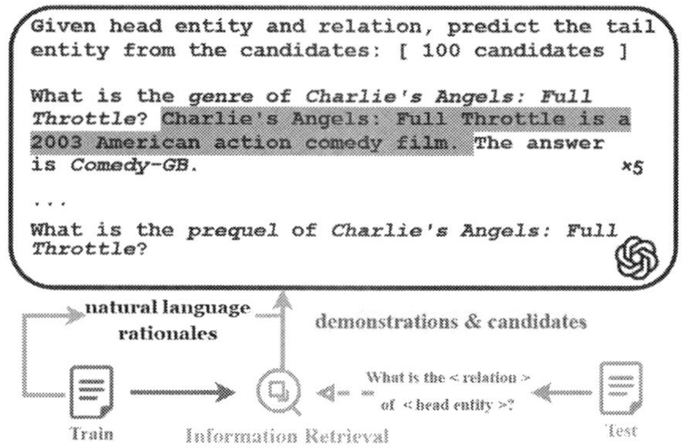

Figure 3: LLM-based KGC. The prompt comprises three components, namely the task description with candidates, demonstrations, and test information.

LLMs We further apply the LLMs, namely GPT-3 and ChatGPT, to assess their effectiveness in KGE (KGC with link prediction). Generative LLMs allow the KGC task to be framed as input sentences containing header entities and relations, making it easier for the model to generate sentences with tail entities. A well-designed prompt can improve the performance of LLMs, and prior studies indicate incorporating in-context learning can improve accuracy and ensure consistent output. Thus, we adopt a similar approach that the prompt comprises three components: task description with candidates, demonstrations, and test information.

As shown in Figure 3, we employ information retrieval (BM25) to select the top 100 most relevant entities from the training set as candidates. Likewise, the prompt's demonstrations utilize the top-5 most similar instances, which assist the model in comprehending the task more effectively. Furthermore, taking inspiration from the Chain-of-

Thought (CoT) method in reasoning tasks, we utilize `natural language rationales` to improve the model's capacity to reason and explain predictions, ultimately improving its overall performance in KGC tasks. Comparatively, the prompt used for ChatGPT solely utilizes a few demonstrations and test data with these strategies.

2.4 Pluggable KGE for Downstream Tasks

We introduce the technical details of applying KGE to downstream tasks as shown in Figure 2. For knowledge graph completion, we feed the model with the textual information $\langle X^h, X^r \rangle$ of the head entity and the relation, then obtain the target tail entity via mask token prediction. For question answering, we feed the model with the question written in natural language concatenated with a `[MASK]` token to obtain the special token of the target answer (entity). For recommendation, we take the user's interaction history as sequential input (Sun et al., 2019) with entity embeddings and then leverage the mask token prediction to obtain recommended items. For the knowledge probing task, we adopt entity embedding as additional knowledge following PELT (Ye et al., 2022).

3 System Usage

The proposed system can be used in three scenarios. First, users can utilize **LambdaKG** to obtain **PLM-based KGE for knowledge discovery**. `LitModel` serves as the training of link prediction task class and fit for all models in Model Hub. Users can choose proper models in `ModelModule` and specific metrics in `DataModule` to train models to obtain the embedding in the KGs. Moreover, users can utilize **LambdaKG PLM-based KGE for downstream tasks**. We provide various prompts to obtain the knowledge (entity) embedding in KGs for downstream tasks. For different tasks, we design different base classes for users to efficiently implement their own tasks. Finally, we provide an online interactive demo for PLM-based KGE at `https://zjunlp.github.io/project/promptkg/demo.html`.

4 Evaluation

4.1 Knowledge Graph Completion

For the KG completion task with small PLMs, we conduct link prediction experiments on two datasets WN18RR (Dettmers et al., 2018), and FB15k-237 (Toutanova et al., 2015). From Table 2, we observe that the discrimination-based method SimKGC (Wang et al., 2022) (previous state-of-the-art) achieves higher performance than other baselines. Generation-based models like KGT5 (Saxena et al., 2022) and GenKGC (Xie et al., 2022) also yield comparable results and show potential abilities in KG representation.

Task	Dataset	Method	hits1	MRR
KG Completion	WN18RR	KG-BERT◇	4.1	21.6
		StAR◇	24.3	40.1
		SimKGC	42.5	60.8
		KGT5	17.9	-
		GenKGC	39.6	-
		kNN-KGE	52.5	57.9
	FB15k-237	KG-BERT◇	-	-
		StAR◇	20.5	29.6
		SimKGC	22.6	30.1
		KGT5	10.8	-
		GenKGC	19.2	-
		kNN-KGE	28.0	37.3
Question Answering	MetaQA	GT query◇	63.3	-
		PullNet◇	65.1	-
		KGT5	67.8	-
Recommendation	ML-20m	BERT4Rec◇	34.4	47.9
		LambdaKG	37.3	50.5
Knowledge Probing	TREx	BERT	28.6	37.7
		RoBERTa	19.9	27.8
		LambdaKG (RoBERTa)	22.1	29.8
	Squad	BERT	13.2	23.5
		RoBERTa	13.4	24.6
		LambdaKG (RoBERTa)	-	-
	Google RE	BERT	10.3	17.3
		RoBERTa	7.6	12.8
		LambdaKG (RoBERTa)	8.1	14.2

Table 2: Hits1 and MRR (%) results on KGC, question answering, recommendation and knowledge probing tasks. ◇ refers to the results from origin papers.

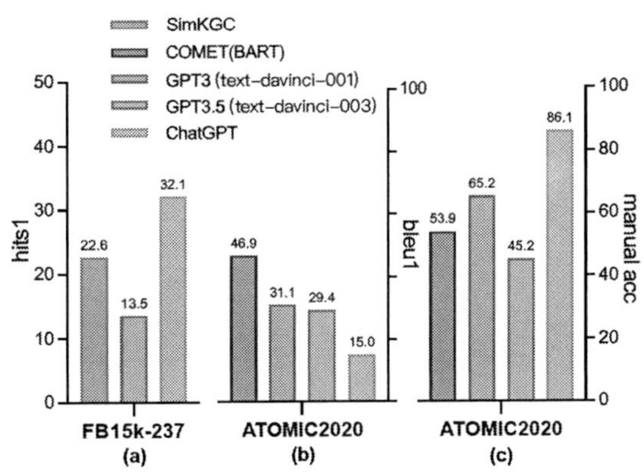

Figure 4: Results on small and large LMs. (a) hit@1 scores on FB15k-237. (b) BLEU-1 scores on ATOMIC2020. (c) Accuracy scores on ATOMIC2020 by manual evaluation.

Small vs. Large LMs We adopt GPT-3/3.5 (`text-davinci-001/003` and ChatGPT) for evaluation and assessment through the interfaces provided by OpenAI. The evaluation of ChatGPT

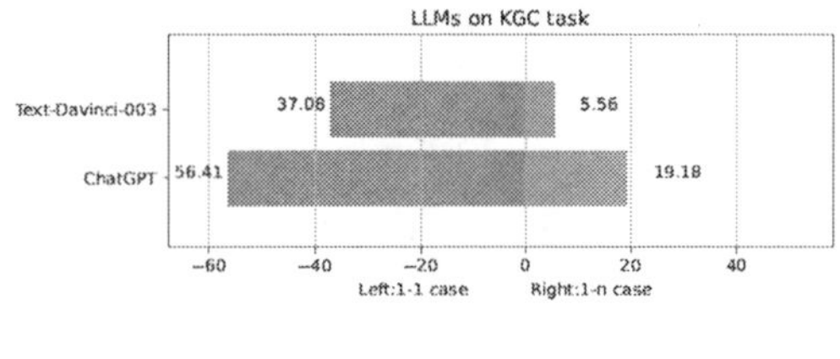

Figure 5: hit@1 of ChatGPT and `text-davinci-003` in FB15k-237.

is conducted on 224 instances, with each relation in the test set. As shown in Figure 4(a), ChatGPT demonstrates better performance, while `text-davinci-003` exhibits a slight gap. The experiment has reaffirmed the capability of LLMs in capturing semantic similarities and regularities among entities, thereby allowing for precise predictions of missing links in knowledge graphs.

In cases where one head entity and relation pair correspond to one or multiple tail entities (1-1 and 1-n cases), we conducted a detailed analysis. Notably, the model performs significantly better in the 1-1 case compared to the 1-n case, as illustrated in Figure 5. Two potential reasons explain this disparity: (1) In the 1-1 case, the model demonstrates a lower propensity for language understanding deviations. Additionally, ChatGPT's training utilizes a larger corpus, enhancing the model to generate accurate responses through analysis and reasoning. (2) The presence of multiple correspondences poses a challenge for the model's capacity to generate informative and contextually relevant responses. Moreover, current evaluation metrics fail to fully capture the intricacy of the responses necessary to properly handle such questions.

We further conduct experiments on **commonsense KG completion** with ATOMIC2020 (Hwang et al., 2021). As suggested in the paper, we sample 5,000 test queries to evaluate the models (excluding ChatGPT). COMET (BART) is fine-tuned through supervised learning and utilizes greedy decoding to generate answers. For GPT3 and ChatGPT, we provide each relation with 5 examples of heads and tails to construct prompts and evaluate them in a zero-shot setting. The results, as shown in Figure 4(b), demonstrates the BLEU-1 scores on the sampled 5,000 queries, while we sample 115 (5 for each relation) queries from the test for ChatGPT. The results indicate that GPT-3 exhibits limited performance in the system evaluation. After analyzing several cases, we sample 115 (5 for each relation) queries as a benchmark and apply manual scoring to evaluate models. Figure 4(c) depicts the accuracy scores of each model. Our study reveals that ChatGPT is capable of generating reasonable outputs, but they are quite different from the ground truth, which accounts for the final results.

4.2 Question Answering

KG is known to be helpful for the task of question answering. We apply **LambdaKG** to question answering and conduct experiments on the MetaQA dataset. Due to computational resource limits, we only evaluate the 1-hop inference performance. From Table 2, KGT5 in **LambdaKG** yields the best performance.

4.3 Recommendation

For the recommendation task, we conduct experiments on a well-established version ML-20m[3]. Linkage of ML-20m and Freebase offered by KB4Rec (Zhao et al., 2019) is utilized to obtain textual descriptions of movies in ML-20m. With movie embeddings pre-trained on these descriptions, we conduct experiments on sequential recommendation tasks following the settings of BERT4Rec (Sun et al., 2019). We notice that **LambdaKG** is confirmed to be effective for the recommendation compared with BERT4Rec.

4.4 Knowledge Probing

Knowledge probing (Petroni et al., 2019) examines the ability of LMs (BERT, RoBERTa, etc.) to recall facts from their parameters. We conduct experiments on LAMA using pre-trained BERT (*bert-base-uncased*) and RoBERTa (*roberta-base*) models. To prove that entity embedding enhanced by KGs helps LMs grab more factual knowledge from PLMs, we train a pluggable entity embedding module following PELT (Ye et al., 2022). As shown in Table 2, the performance boosts while we use the entity embedding module.

5 Conclusion and Future Work

We propose **LambdaKG**, a library that establishes a unified toolkit with well-defined modules and easy-to-use interfaces to support research on using PLMs on KGs. In the future, we will continue to integrate more models and tasks (e.g., dialogue) into the proposed library to facilitate the research progress of the KG.

[3] `https://grouplens.org/datasets/movielens/20m/`

Acknowledgment

We would like to express our heartfelt gratitude to the anonymous reviewers for their thoughtful and kind comments. This work was supported by the National Natural Science Foundation of China (No.62206246), Zhejiang Provincial Natural Science Foundation of China (No. LGG22F030011), Ningbo Natural Science Foundation (2021J190), Yongjiang Talent Introduction Programme (2021A-156-G).

References

Mehdi Ali, Max Berrendorf, Charles Tapley Hoyt, Laurent Vermue, Sahand Sharifzadeh, Volker Tresp, and Jens Lehmann. 2021. Pykeen 1.0: A python library for training and evaluating knowledge graph embeddings. *J. Mach. Learn. Res.*, 22:82:1–82:6.

Antoine Bordes, Nicolas Usunier, Alberto García-Durán, Jason Weston, and Oksana Yakhnenko. 2013. Translating embeddings for modeling multi-relational data. In *Advances in Neural Information Processing Systems 26: 27th Annual Conference on Neural Information Processing Systems 2013. Proceedings of a meeting held December 5-8, 2013, Lake Tahoe, Nevada, United States*, pages 2787–2795.

Samuel Broscheit, Daniel Ruffinelli, Adrian Kochsiek, Patrick Betz, and Rainer Gemulla. 2020. Libkge - A knowledge graph embedding library for reproducible research. In *Proceedings of the 2020 Conference on Empirical Methods in Natural Language Processing: System Demonstrations, EMNLP 2020 - Demos, Online, November 16-20, 2020*, pages 165–174. Association for Computational Linguistics.

Tom B. Brown, Benjamin Mann, Nick Ryder, Melanie Subbiah, Jared Kaplan, Prafulla Dhariwal, Arvind Neelakantan, Pranav Shyam, Girish Sastry, Amanda Askell, Sandhini Agarwal, Ariel Herbert-Voss, Gretchen Krueger, Tom Henighan, Rewon Child, Aditya Ramesh, Daniel M. Ziegler, Jeffrey Wu, Clemens Winter, Christopher Hesse, Mark Chen, Eric Sigler, Mateusz Litwin, Scott Gray, Benjamin Chess, Jack Clark, Christopher Berner, Sam McCandlish, Alec Radford, Ilya Sutskever, and Dario Amodei. 2020. Language models are few-shot learners. In *Advances in Neural Information Processing Systems 33: Annual Conference on Neural Information Processing Systems 2020, NeurIPS 2020, December 6-12, 2020, virtual*.

Chen Chen, Yufei Wang, Bing Li, and Kwok-Yan Lam. 2022a. Knowledge is flat: A seq2seq generative framework for various knowledge graph completion. In *Proceedings of the 29th International Conference on Computational Linguistics, COLING 2022, Gyeongju, Republic of Korea, October 12-17, 2022*, pages 4005–4017. International Committee on Computational Linguistics.

Xiang Chen, Ningyu Zhang, Xin Xie, Shumin Deng, Yunzhi Yao, Chuanqi Tan, Fei Huang, Luo Si, and Huajun Chen. 2022b. Knowprompt: Knowledge-aware prompt-tuning with synergistic optimization for relation extraction. In *WWW '22: The ACM Web Conference 2022, Virtual Event, Lyon, France, April 25 - 29, 2022*, pages 2778–2788. ACM.

Tim Dettmers, Pasquale Minervini, Pontus Stenetorp, and Sebastian Riedel. 2018. Convolutional 2d knowledge graph embeddings. In *Proceedings of the Thirty-Second AAAI Conference on Artificial Intelligence, (AAAI-18), the 30th innovative Applications of Artificial Intelligence (IAAI-18), and the 8th AAAI Symposium on Educational Advances in Artificial Intelligence (EAAI-18), New Orleans, Louisiana, USA, February 2-7, 2018*, pages 1811–1818. AAAI Press.

Jacob Devlin, Ming-Wei Chang, Kenton Lee, and Kristina Toutanova. 2018. BERT: pre-training of deep bidirectional transformers for language understanding. *CoRR*, abs/1810.04805.

Xu Han, Shulin Cao, Xin Lv, Yankai Lin, Zhiyuan Liu, Maosong Sun, and Juanzi Li. 2018. Openke: An open toolkit for knowledge embedding. In *Proceedings of the 2018 Conference on Empirical Methods in Natural Language Processing, EMNLP 2018: System Demonstrations, Brussels, Belgium, October 31 - November 4, 2018*, pages 139–144. Association for Computational Linguistics.

Jena D. Hwang, Chandra Bhagavatula, Ronan Le Bras, Jeff Da, Keisuke Sakaguchi, Antoine Bosselut, and Yejin Choi. 2021. (comet-) atomic 2020: On symbolic and neural commonsense knowledge graphs. In *Thirty-Fifth AAAI Conference on Artificial Intelligence, AAAI 2021, Thirty-Third Conference on Innovative Applications of Artificial Intelligence, IAAI 2021, The Eleventh Symposium on Educational Advances in Artificial Intelligence, EAAI 2021, Virtual Event, February 2-9, 2021*, pages 6384–6392. AAAI Press.

Zhuoran Jin, Tianyi Men, Hongbang Yuan, Zhitao He, Dianbo Sui, Chenhao Wang, Zhipeng Xue, Yubo Chen, and Jun Zhao. 2022. Cogkge: A knowledge graph embedding toolkit and benchmark for representing multi-source and heterogeneous knowledge. In *Proceedings of the 60th Annual Meeting of the Association for Computational Linguistics, ACL 2022 - System Demonstrations, Dublin, Ireland, May 22-27, 2022*, pages 166–173. Association for Computational Linguistics.

Bosung Kim, Taesuk Hong, Youngjoong Ko, and Jungyun Seo. 2020. Multi-task learning for knowledge graph completion with pre-trained language models. In *Proceedings of the 28th International Conference on Computational Linguistics*, pages 1737–1743, Barcelona, Spain (Online). International Committee on Computational Linguistics.

Mike Lewis, Yinhan Liu, Naman Goyal, Marjan Ghazvininejad, Abdelrahman Mohamed, Omer Levy,

Veselin Stoyanov, and Luke Zettlemoyer. 2020. BART: denoising sequence-to-sequence pre-training for natural language generation, translation, and comprehension. In *Proceedings of the 58th Annual Meeting of the Association for Computational Linguistics, ACL 2020, Online, July 5-10, 2020*, pages 7871–7880. Association for Computational Linguistics.

Xiao Liu, Shiyu Zhao, Kai Su, Yukuo Cen, Jiezhong Qiu, Mengdi Zhang, Wei Wu, Yuxiao Dong, and Jie Tang. 2022. Mask and reason: Pre-training knowledge graph transformers for complex logical queries. In *KDD '22: The 28th ACM SIGKDD Conference on Knowledge Discovery and Data Mining, Washington, DC, USA, August 14 - 18, 2022*, pages 1120–1130. ACM.

Ye Liu, Yao Wan, Lifang He, Hao Peng, and Philip S. Yu. 2021. KG-BART: knowledge graph-augmented BART for generative commonsense reasoning. In *Thirty-Fifth AAAI Conference on Artificial Intelligence, AAAI 2021, Thirty-Third Conference on Innovative Applications of Artificial Intelligence, IAAI 2021, The Eleventh Symposium on Educational Advances in Artificial Intelligence, EAAI 2021, Virtual Event, February 2-9, 2021*, pages 6418–6425. AAAI Press.

Xin Lv, Yankai Lin, Yixin Cao, Lei Hou, Juanzi Li, Zhiyuan Liu, Peng Li, and Jie Zhou. 2022. Do pretrained models benefit knowledge graph completion? A reliable evaluation and a reasonable approach. In *Findings of the Association for Computational Linguistics: ACL 2022, Dublin, Ireland, May 22-27, 2022*, pages 3570–3581. Association for Computational Linguistics.

Elan Markowitz, Keshav Balasubramanian, Mehrnoosh Mirtaheri, Murali Annavaram, Aram Galstyan, and Greg Ver Steeg. 2022. StATIK: Structure and text for inductive knowledge graph completion. In *Findings of the Association for Computational Linguistics: NAACL 2022*, pages 604–615, Seattle, United States. Association for Computational Linguistics.

OpenAI. 2022. Chatgpt: Optimizing language models for dialogue. `https://openai.com/blog/chatgpt/`.

Fabio Petroni, Tim Rocktäschel, Sebastian Riedel, Patrick S. H. Lewis, Anton Bakhtin, Yuxiang Wu, and Alexander H. Miller. 2019. Language models as knowledge bases? In *Proceedings of the 2019 Conference on Empirical Methods in Natural Language Processing and the 9th International Joint Conference on Natural Language Processing, EMNLP-IJCNLP 2019, Hong Kong, China, November 3-7, 2019*, pages 2463–2473. Association for Computational Linguistics.

Colin Raffel, Noam Shazeer, Adam Roberts, Katherine Lee, Sharan Narang, Michael Matena, Yanqi Zhou, Wei Li, and Peter J. Liu. 2020. Exploring the limits of transfer learning with a unified text-to-text transformer. *J. Mach. Learn. Res.*, 21:140:1–140:67.

Apoorv Saxena, Adrian Kochsiek, and Rainer Gemulla. 2022. Sequence-to-sequence knowledge graph completion and question answering. In *Proceedings of the 60th Annual Meeting of the Association for Computational Linguistics (Volume 1: Long Papers), ACL 2022, Dublin, Ireland, May 22-27, 2022*, pages 2814–2828. Association for Computational Linguistics.

Fei Sun, Jun Liu, Jian Wu, Changhua Pei, Xiao Lin, Wenwu Ou, and Peng Jiang. 2019. Bert4rec: Sequential recommendation with bidirectional encoder representations from transformer. In *Proceedings of the 28th ACM International Conference on Information and Knowledge Management, CIKM 2019, Beijing, China, November 3-7, 2019*, pages 1441–1450. ACM.

Kristina Toutanova, Danqi Chen, Patrick Pantel, Hoifung Poon, Pallavi Choudhury, and Michael Gamon. 2015. Representing text for joint embedding of text and knowledge bases. In *Proceedings of the 2015 Conference on Empirical Methods in Natural Language Processing, EMNLP 2015, Lisbon, Portugal, September 17-21, 2015*, pages 1499–1509. The Association for Computational Linguistics.

Bo Wang, Tao Shen, Guodong Long, Tianyi Zhou, Ying Wang, and Yi Chang. 2021. Structure-augmented text representation learning for efficient knowledge graph completion. In *WWW '21: The Web Conference 2021, Virtual Event / Ljubljana, Slovenia, April 19-23, 2021*, pages 1737–1748. ACM / IW3C2.

Liang Wang, Wei Zhao, Zhuoyu Wei, and Jingming Liu. 2022. Simkgc: Simple contrastive knowledge graph completion with pre-trained language models. In *Proceedings of the 60th Annual Meeting of the Association for Computational Linguistics (Volume 1: Long Papers), ACL 2022, Dublin, Ireland, May 22-27, 2022*, pages 4281–4294. Association for Computational Linguistics.

Xin Xie, Ningyu Zhang, Zhoubo Li, Shumin Deng, Hui Chen, Feiyu Xiong, Mosha Chen, and Huajun Chen. 2022. From discrimination to generation: Knowledge graph completion with generative transformer. In *Companion of The Web Conference 2022, Virtual Event / Lyon, France, April 25 - 29, 2022*, pages 162–165. ACM.

Liang Yao, Chengsheng Mao, and Yuan Luo. 2019. KG-BERT: BERT for knowledge graph completion. *CoRR*, abs/1909.03193.

Deming Ye, Yankai Lin, Peng Li, Maosong Sun, and Zhiyuan Liu. 2022. A simple but effective pluggable entity lookup table for pre-trained language models. In *Proceedings of the 60th Annual Meeting of the Association for Computational Linguistics (Volume 2: Short Papers), ACL 2022, Dublin, Ireland, May 22-27, 2022*, pages 523–529. Association for Computational Linguistics.

Ningyu Zhang, Qianghuai Jia, Shumin Deng, Xiang Chen, Hongbin Ye, Hui Chen, Huaixiao Tou, Gang

Huang, Zhao Wang, Nengwei Hua, and Huajun Chen. 2021. Alicg: Fine-grained and evolvable conceptual graph construction for semantic search at alibaba. In *KDD '21: The 27th ACM SIGKDD Conference on Knowledge Discovery and Data Mining, Virtual Event, Singapore, August 14-18, 2021*, pages 3895–3905. ACM.

Ningyu Zhang, Xin Xie, Xiang Chen, Shumin Deng, Chuanqi Tan, Fei Huang, Xu Cheng, and Huajun Chen. 2022a. Reasoning through memorization: Nearest neighbor knowledge graph embeddings. *CoRR*, abs/2201.05575.

Ningyu Zhang, Xin Xu, Liankuan Tao, Haiyang Yu, Hongbin Ye, Shuofei Qiao, Xin Xie, Xiang Chen, Zhoubo Li, Lei Li, et al. 2022b. Deepke: A deep learning based knowledge extraction toolkit for knowledge base population. In *Proceedings of EMNLP Demonstration*.

Wen Zhang, Xiangnan Chen, Zhen Yao, Mingyang Chen, Yushan Zhu, Hongtao Yu, Yufeng Huang, Yajing Xu, Ningyu Zhang, Zezhong Xu, Zonggang Yuan, Feiyu Xiong, and Huajun Chen. 2022c. Neuralkg: An open source library for diverse representation learning of knowledge graphs. In *SIGIR*, pages 3323–3328. ACM.

Wayne Xin Zhao, Gaole He, Kunlin Yang, Hongjian Dou, Jin Huang, Siqi Ouyang, and Ji-Rong Wen. 2019. Kb4rec: A data set for linking knowledge bases with recommender systems. *Data Intell.*, 1(2):121–136.

mahaNLP: A Marathi Natural Language Processing Library

Vidula Magdum[1,3], Omkar Dhekane[1,3], Sharayu Hiwarkhedkar[1,3], Saloni Mittal[1,3]
Raviraj Joshi[2,3]
[1] Pune Institute of Computer Technology, Pune, Maharashtra India
[2] Indian Institute of Technology Madras, Chennai, Tamil Nadu India
[3] L3Cube Pune
{vidulamagdum12, omkarjd1212, hiwarkhedkarsharayu, salonimittal12}@gmail.com
ravirajoshi@gmail.com

Abstract

We present mahaNLP, an open-source natural language processing (NLP) library specifically built for the Marathi language. It aims to enhance the support for the low-resource Indian language Marathi in the field of NLP. It is an easy-to-use, extensible, and modular toolkit for Marathi text analysis built on state-of-the-art MahaBERT-based transformer models. Our work holds significant importance as other existing Indic NLP libraries provide basic Marathi processing support and rely on older models with restricted performance. Our toolkit stands out by offering a comprehensive array of NLP tasks, encompassing both fundamental preprocessing tasks and advanced NLP tasks like sentiment analysis, NER, hate speech detection, and sentence completion. This paper focuses on an overview of the mahaNLP framework, its features, and its usage. This work is a part of the L3Cube MahaNLP initiative, more information about it can be found at https://github.com/l3cube-pune/MarathiNLP.

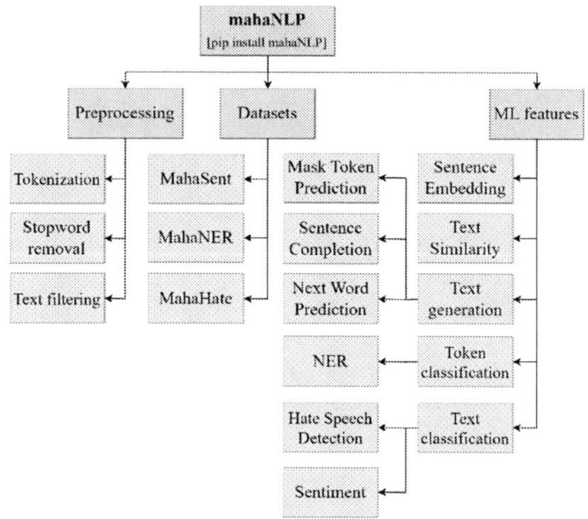

Figure 1: A brief overview of the features in mahaNLP library

1 Introduction

Natural Language Processing (NLP) is a major subset of artificial intelligence. It helps to clear up linguistic ambiguity and gives the data a useful quantitative structure for numerous downstream tasks. While NLP has the potential to have a huge impact on the ML community, recent models have primarily focused on English and 6 other languages[1] with a significantly high amount of resources (Joshi et al., 2020). There are around 7,000 languages spoken worldwide[2]. Out of which, approximately 22+ languages are existing Indian languages[3] that are widely spoken not only in India but also throughout the world. Developing models that work for these languages is important for a variety of reasons, including bridging the existing language divide and promoting exploration and research for non-English languages in the growing NLP field[4].

The Marathi language is 11th in the list of popular languages across the globe[5]. Despite being a widely spoken language, Marathi-specific NLP monolingual resources are still limited in comparison to other natural languages (Joshi, 2022a). There are many popular open-source tools like Spacy[6], Stanza[7], iNLTK[8], IndicNLP (Kunchukuttan, 2020), providing features to create effective multilingual NLP systems. Though these libraries do support the multilingual functionality for Marathi, they are not exhaustive with respect to the functionalities they support and have their own set of limitations and discrepancies, such as the usage of older architectures to implement multilingual models (Ruder et al., 2021). Basic

[1] https://datasaur.ai/blog-posts/nlp-work-in-different-languages

[2] https://en.wikipedia.org/wiki/Lists_of_languages

[3] https://en.wikipedia.org/wiki/Languages_of_India

[4] https://ruder.io/state-of-multilingual-ai/index.html

[5] https://en.wikipedia.org/wiki/Marathi_language

[6] https://spacy.io/

[7] https://stanfordnlp.github.io/stanza/

[8] https://inltk.readthedocs.io/en/latest/

Proceedings of the 13th International Joint Conference on Natural Language Processing and the 3rd Conference of the Asia-Pacific Chapter of the Association for Computational Linguistics: System Demonstrations, pages 34–40

	Lemmatization	Part of Speech Tagging	Dependency Parsing	Multi- word token expansion	Sentence Segmentation	Sentence Embedding	Remove Foreign Languages	Sentence Similarity	Sentiment Analysis	Hate Speech Detection	Named Entity Recognition	Next Token Prediction
iNLTK						✓	✓	✓				✓
Stanza	✓	✓	✓	✓	✓						✓	✓
spaCy					✓	✓		✓				
mahaNLP					✓	✓	✓	✓	✓	✓	✓	✓

Figure 2: A comparison of a few existing libraries and mahaNLP specific to the Marathi language

features like Marathi sentiment analysis, named entity recognition, and hate speech detection is missing in almost all the current multilingual libraries. Additionally, the absence of out-of-the-box features present in other libraries (yet served by L3Cube-mahaNLP library) makes it difficult for the comparative analysis of these models.

The L3Cube-MahaNLP[9] (Joshi, 2022b) initiative is an umbrella for various tools, datasets, and models that greatly assist in Marathi language processing. With this work, we aim to provide a broader set of functionalities to developers. In this paper, we propose mahaNLP library - a python-based NLP toolkit focused on the Indian language Marathi and majorly built on top of Hugging Face transformer models[10]. Along with basic language processing features, the open-source toolkit wraps the state-of-the-art monolingual Marathi transformer models for text analysis. It encompasses a myriad of features like sentiment and hate analysis, named entity recognition, and a variety of other Marathi language processing features as shown in Figure 1. Thus, the mahaNLP library aims to make Marathi NLP more accessible. The demonstration video[11] and example colab[12] are shared publicly.

2 Related Work

The communities of NLP and machine learning have a prolonged history of developing open-source tools and libraries. There are numerous user-friendly, all-purpose NLP libraries available. NLTK (Bird, 2006), Stanford CoreNLP (Manning et al., 2014), Spacy (Honnibal and Montani, 2017), AllenNLP (Gardner et al., 2018), Flair (Akbik et al., 2019), Stanza (Qi et al., 2020), Hugging Face Transformers (Wolf et al., 2019) and iNLTK (Arora, 2020) are some of the libraries that are primarily concerned with NLP tasks. These libraries provide NLP tasks to the ML community like tokenization, sentence encoding, text normalization, translation, and so on.

However, while some of these libraries do support Marathi, they have a very limited range of NLP tasks and pre-trained language models. Figure 2 illustrates the provisional comparison between mahaNLP and the existing libraries for the language Marathi. The iNLTK library is not actively supported, it is based on very limited datasets and LSTM-based ULMFiT models. Marathi models for features like sentiment and NER are unavailable in SpaCy. MahaNLP attempts to address these issues by offering a broader set of pre-trained language models, including BERT (Devlin et al., 2018), RoBERTa (Liu et al., 2019), and AlBERT (Lan et al., 2019), as well as a broader set of NLP tasks such as sentiment analysis, hate speech analysis, NER Tagger, and MLM-based modules. The NER model supported by Stanza is based on our L3Cube-MahaNER corpus (Litake et al., 2022)[13].

3 System Design and Architecture

The *ease-of-access* is an important characteristic of mahaNLP and the system is designed from the user's perspective. These perspectives can be mainly defined as - a *Standard Flow* and a *Model Flow*.

3.1 Standard Flow

The *Standard Flow* can be used by a basic programmer who has the least knowledge of the machine learning domain. In this flow, the complex model arguments are isolated from the users. They can use a feature without knowledge of the models used in the background. This flow has constructs similar to standard NLP libraries. The intuitive nature of this flow makes mahaNLP more user-friendly and easily accessible. The pre-processing,

[9] `https://github.com/l3cube-pune/MarathiNLP`

[10] `https://huggingface.co/l3cube-pune`

[11] `https://youtu.be/KxExcwCrTO0`

[12] Example colab

[13] `https://stanfordnlp.github.io/stanza/ner_models.html`

tokenizer, datasets, and ML-based models are part of this user flow.

3.1.1 Pre-process Module

An initial step in any NLP task is the preprocessing of data. The transformer models in NLP perform much better on cleaned data than raw, unprocessed corpus. The preprocess module helps to provide functions such as the removal of URLs, stopwords, and non-Devanagari words for cleaning Marathi textual data.

3.1.2 Tokenizer Module

A very important step in many NLP tasks is the tokenization of text. The mahaNLP Tokenizer module provides functionalities for sentence-level tokenization (splitting into multiple sentences) and word-level tokenization (splitting into multiple words).

3.1.3 Datasets Module

The mahaNLP library currently supports 3 datasets - MahaHate (Patil et al., 2022) for hate speech detection, MahaSent (Kulkarni et al., 2021) (Pingle et al., 2023) for sentiment analysis, and MahaNER (Litake et al., 2022) for named entity recognition. These datasets can mainly be used for finetuning tasks. These datasets are given as-is in our library and have an official train-test-valid split. Each of these corpora can be separately loaded in the pandas data frame. The datasets are cached locally to avoid repeated downloads.

Feature name	Labels / Outputs	Function name(s)
Sentiment	positive, negative, neutral	get_polarity_score
Hate	hate, non-hate	get_hate_score
Tagger	Person (NEP), Location (NEL), Organization (NEO), Measure (NEM), Time (NETI), Date (NED), Designation (ED)	get_token_labels, get_tokens
Auto Complete	next (N) words	next_word, complete_sentence
Mask Fill	masked word	predict_mask
Similarity	similarity score (0-1)	embed_sentences, get_similarity_score

Table 1: Standard Flow ML features

3.1.4 Machine learning-based modules

A set of modules utilizes machine learning models in the background to provide the desired functionality. Currently, these features or modules are implemented using state-of-the-art Marathi Transformer models and are described below. The basic syntax to use them is:

```
module_name = Module()
result = module_name.functionality_name(text)
```

Table 1 shows the features supported, output type, and the corresponding functions.

3.2 Model Flow

The *Model Flow* provides advanced functionality intended for use by ML practitioners with knowledge in the NLP domain. It offers flexibility for programmers to select background models and adjust their parameters. The *model_repo* module defines the model flow. Table 2 presents the association between standard flow machine learning-based modules and *model_repo* submodules. It also reports the accuracy/F1 scores for pertinent features on the benchmark test sets.

4 System Usage

The mahaNLP library is hosted on the official PyPI repository. It can be installed using the pip command:

```
pip install mahaNLP
```

Once installed, we can then import the required features using the python import statement and start utilizing various functionalities. Currently, the library has been tested on x64-bit Windows 10 OS and Google Colab platform (posix-linux).

4.1 Dataset Loading

A snippet of code demonstrating the loading *mahaSent* dataset provided by mahaNLP is given below:

```
# import
from mahaNLP.datasets import *

# loadDatasets: This loads the dataset into our variable
# parameter:
# name of the dataset

dataset = load_datasets('mahaSent')
```

Standard Flow Module	model_repo submodule	Huggingface model	Score(Acc/F1)
sentiment	SentimentModel	marathi-sentiment-md (Pingle et al., 2023)	84.90
hate	HateModel	mahahate-bert (Patil et al., 2022)	90.9
tagger	NERModel	marathi-ner (Litake et al., 2022)	86.8
autocomplete	GPTModel	marathi-gpt (Joshi, 2022a)	-
mask_fill	MaskFillModel	marathi-bert-v2 (Joshi, 2022a)	-
similarity	SimilarityModel	marathi-sentence-similarity-sbert (Joshi et al., 2022)	83

Table 2: Table shows which *model_repo* submodules are inherited by the Standard Flow modules and the default huggingface model internally used. The huggingface models can be listed and selected in the Model Flow. The score column indicates the accuracy of the model on standard test sets as reported in original works. The scoring metric of the sentiment and hate model is accuracy while that of the NER and similarity model is F1-score and embedding similarity score respectively.

4.2 Usage via Standard Flow

In *Standard Flow*, the user can simply import the feature they want to use (e.g. autocomplete, sentiment, tagger, etc.) and define the object to initialize that particular model. Here, the user can optionally pass the *model_name* as an argument during model initialization.
A simple snippet of generic flow usage for *SentimentAnalyzer* class object is given below:

```
# import
from mahaNLP.sentiment import SentimentAnalyzer

# create a model object
model = SentimentAnalyzer()

# function - getPolarityScore
# It gives the sentiment score in the range of 0 to 1
# for 3 poles: Neutral, Positive, Negative

# example:
text = 'दिवाळीच्या सणादरम्यान सगळे आनंदी असतात.'
# English Translation:
# 'Everyone is happy during Diwali festival.'

polarscore = model.get_polarity_score(text)
print(polarscore)
```

```
     label     score
0  Positive  0.995338
```

The *get_polarity_score* function returns *float* value representing the confidence score for a predicted sentiment class.

4.3 Usage via Model Flow

In *Model Flow*, the user has to import the specific model (e.g. mahaHate, mahaNER, etc.) using import mahanlp.model_repo.modelname. Then, the user can define the model object and also can optionally pass the *model_name* as an argument. Refer the following code for loading and usage of the *MaskFillModel* class object via *Model Flow*.

```
# import
from mahaNLP.model_repo import MaskFillModel

# create a model object
# parameter:
# model name
model = MaskFillModel('marathi-bert-v2')

# function - predictMask
# It predictes the masked token

text = 'मी महाराष्ट्रात [MASK].'
# English Translation:
# 'I in Maharashtra [MASK]'

# parameters:
# text, details of prediction, print in dict

model.predict_mask(text, details = "all", as_dict = False)
```

The predicted token string, sequence, and score can be returned as:

	score	token	token_str	sequence
0	0.465607	1155	आहे	मी महाराष्ट्रात आहे.
1	0.079688	92222	राहणार	मी महाराष्ट्रात राहणार.
2	0.074000	1826	नाही	मी महाराष्ट्रात नाही.
3	0.050423	1617	##च	मी महाराष्ट्रातच.
4	0.043737	62560	राहतो	मी महाराष्ट्रात राहतो.

The library also supports various standard hardware devices. The *gpu_enabled = True* option allows users to utilize the gpu for model usage or inference.

Table 3 demonstrates all the modules of MahaNLP along with inputs and their expected outputs. The detailed description and usage of all the functionalities in mahaNLP are available at the **mahaNLP PyPI project**.

5 Conclusion and Future Work

We have built mahaNLP - a simple, easy-to-use and extensible toolkit for Marathi language pro-

Functionality	**Models Used**	**Input**	**Output**
Sentiment Analysis	marathi-sentiment-md	दिवाळीच्या सणादरम्यान सगळे आनंदी असतात. (Everyone is happy during Diwali festival.)	**Label**:Positive **Score**: 0.995
Hate Analysis	mahahate-bert mahahate-multi-roberta	ती मूर्ख आहे. मला ती आवडत नाही. (She is stupid. I don't like her.)	**Label**:Hate **Score**:0.966
Masked Token Prediction	marathi-bert-v2 marathi-roberta marathi-albert	मी महाराष्ट्रात [MASK].	मी महाराष्ट्रात **राहतो**. (I live in Maharashtra)
Autocomplete	marathi-gpt	आज खूप पाऊस. (A lot of rain today)	आज खूप पाऊस पडला होता. यामुळे ही समस्या गंभीर बनली आहे. (It rained a lot today. That's why this problem has gotten serious)
Sentence Similarity	marathi-sentence-similarity-sbert marathi-sentence-bert-nli	**Source Text**: त्याला पाकिटात हजार रुपये मिळाले. (He found 1000 rupees in his wallet.) **Target Text**: त्याला पाकिटात काही पैसे सापडले. (He found some cash in his wallet.)	**Similarity**: 0.781
Entity Recognition	marathi-ner	१७ तारखेला आदित्य पुण्यात आला. (Aditya came to Pune on 17th.)	Date Other Person Location Other

Table 3: Sample examples of features provided by mahaNLP

cessing and development of robust NLP models. The mahaNLP is majorly built on the top of the huggingface transformers[14] library and utilizes pyTorch[15] framework under the hood. It also utilizes the resources developed by L3Cube as a part of MahaNLP initiative. It primarily provides wrapper classes to perform downstream tasks on supervised datasets, transformer models, and other tools for natural language processing in Marathi. The paper demonstrates the usage of various modules in the mahaNLP library.

We are working on expanding our project scope in the following manner:

- Expanding the project to support more low-resource Indic languages.
- Extending the existing corpora provided by the library and supporting Indo-Aryan language datasets and other regional language datasets like Konkani and Dongari which are very prevalent in Maharashtra state.
- Addition of pretrained models for advanced downstream tasks like machine translation, natural language inference etc.
- Creation of web-based user interactive tools or APIs which can be used by developers at the production level.
- Further improvements in model accuracy for predictions and reduction in overall model size and computational cost.

Limitations

- Pre-processing can be made more efficient by expanding the dataset for stopwords to a more exhaustive list.
- The state-of-art huggingface transformer models have not been tested on a generic domain, but only on specific domains such as the news or social media domain. More generic models built as a part of a broader initiative will be integrated into the library.

[14]https://huggingface.co/l3cube-pune
[15]https://pytorch.org/

- The current language models provided by mahaNLP are built on transformers that have high runtime on CPU. In the future, we plan to build and integrate more compact models.

These issues are planned to be addressed in the upcoming versions of the library.

References

Alan Akbik, Tanja Bergmann, Duncan Blythe, Kashif Rasul, Stefan Schweter, and Roland Vollgraf. 2019. Flair: An easy-to-use framework for state-of-the-art nlp. In *Proceedings of the 2019 conference of the North American chapter of the association for computational linguistics (demonstrations)*, pages 54–59.

Gaurav Arora. 2020. inltk: Natural language toolkit for indic languages. *arXiv preprint arXiv:2009.12534*.

Steven Bird. 2006. Nltk: the natural language toolkit. In *Proceedings of the COLING/ACL 2006 Interactive Presentation Sessions*, pages 69–72.

Jacob Devlin, Ming-Wei Chang, Kenton Lee, and Kristina Toutanova. 2018. Bert: Pre-training of deep bidirectional transformers for language understanding. *arXiv preprint arXiv:1810.04805*.

Matt Gardner, Joel Grus, Mark Neumann, Oyvind Tafjord, Pradeep Dasigi, Nelson Liu, Matthew Peters, Michael Schmitz, and Luke Zettlemoyer. 2018. Allennlp: A deep semantic natural language processing platform. *arXiv preprint arXiv:1803.07640*.

Matthew Honnibal and Ines Montani. 2017. spacy 2: Natural language understanding with bloom embeddings, convolutional neural networks and incremental parsing. *To appear*, 7(1):411–420.

Ananya Joshi, Aditi Kajale, Janhavi Gadre, Samruddhi Deode, and Raviraj Joshi. 2022. L3cube-mahasbert and hindsbert: Sentence bert models and benchmarking bert sentence representations for hindi and marathi. *arXiv preprint arXiv:2211.11187*.

Pratik Joshi, Sebastin Santy, Amar Budhiraja, Kalika Bali, and Monojit Choudhury. 2020. The state and fate of linguistic diversity and inclusion in the nlp world. In *Proceedings of the 58th Annual Meeting of the Association for Computational Linguistics*, pages 6282–6293.

Raviraj Joshi. 2022a. L3Cube-MahaCorpus and MahaBERT: Marathi monolingual corpus, Marathi BERT language models, and resources. In *Proceedings of the WILDRE-6 Workshop within the 13th Language Resources and Evaluation Conference*, pages 97–101, Marseille, France. European Language Resources Association.

Raviraj Joshi. 2022b. L3cube-mahanlp: Marathi natural language processing datasets, models, and library. *arXiv preprint arXiv:2205.14728*.

Atharva Kulkarni, Meet Mandhane, Manali Likhitkar, Gayatri Kshirsagar, and Raviraj Joshi. 2021. L3cubemahasent: A marathi tweet-based sentiment analysis dataset. In *Proceedings of the Eleventh Workshop on Computational Approaches to Subjectivity, Sentiment and Social Media Analysis*, pages 213–220.

Anoop Kunchukuttan. 2020. The IndicNLP Library. `https://github.com/anoopkunchukuttan/indic_nlp_library/blob/master/docs/indicnlp.pdf`.

Zhenzhong Lan, Mingda Chen, Sebastian Goodman, Kevin Gimpel, Piyush Sharma, and Radu Soricut. 2019. Albert: A lite bert for self-supervised learning of language representations. *arXiv preprint arXiv:1909.11942*.

Onkar Litake, Maithili Ravindra Sabane, Parth Sachin Patil, Aparna Abhijeet Ranade, and Raviraj Joshi. 2022. L3cube-mahaner: A marathi named entity recognition dataset and bert models. In *Proceedings of The WILDRE-6 Workshop within the 13th Language Resources and Evaluation Conference*, pages 29–34, Marseille, France. European Language Resources Association.

Yinhan Liu, Myle Ott, Naman Goyal, Jingfei Du, Mandar Joshi, Danqi Chen, Omer Levy, Mike Lewis, Luke Zettlemoyer, and Veselin Stoyanov. 2019. Roberta: A robustly optimized bert pretraining approach. *arXiv preprint arXiv:1907.11692*.

Christopher D Manning, Mihai Surdeanu, John Bauer, Jenny Rose Finkel, Steven Bethard, and David McClosky. 2014. The stanford corenlp natural language processing toolkit. In *Proceedings of 52nd annual meeting of the association for computational linguistics: system demonstrations*, pages 55–60.

Hrushikesh Patil, Abhishek Velankar, and Raviraj Joshi. 2022. L3cube-mahahate: A tweet-based marathi hate speech detection dataset and bert models. In *Proceedings of the Third Workshop on Threat, Aggression and Cyberbullying (TRAC 2022)*, pages 1–9.

Aabha Pingle, Aditya Vyawahare, Isha Joshi, Rahul Tangsali, and Raviraj Joshi. 2023. L3cube-mahasent-md: A multi-domain marathi sentiment analysis dataset and transformer models. *arXiv preprint arXiv:2306.13888*.

Peng Qi, Yuhao Zhang, Yuhui Zhang, Jason Bolton, and Christopher D Manning. 2020. Stanza: A python natural language processing toolkit for many human languages. *arXiv preprint arXiv:2003.07082*.

Sebastian Ruder, Noah Constant, Jan Botha, Aditya Siddhant, Orhan Firat, Jinlan Fu, Pengfei Liu, Junjie Hu, Dan Garrette, Graham Neubig, et al. 2021. Xtreme-r: Towards more challenging and nuanced multilingual evaluation. In *Proceedings of the 2021 Conference on Empirical Methods in Natural Language Processing*, pages 10215–10245.

Thomas Wolf, Lysandre Debut, Victor Sanh, Julien Chaumond, Clement Delangue, Anthony Moi, Pierric Cistac, Tim Rault, Rémi Louf, Morgan Funtowicz, et al. 2019. Huggingface's transformers: State-of-the-art natural language processing. *arXiv preprint arXiv:1910.03771*.

SAINE: Scientific Annotation and Inference Engine

Susie Xi Rao[1], **Yilei Tu**[2], **Peter H. Egger**[3]
[1] Chair of Applied Economics; Institute of Computing Platforms, ETH Zurich
[2] Chair of Applied Economics; Department of Computer Science, ETH Zurich
[3] Chair of Applied Economics, ETH Zurich; CEPR; CESifo
{srao, yiletu, pegger}@ethz.ch

Abstract

We present **SAINE**, a **S**cientific **A**nnotation and **I**nference **EN**gine based on a set of standard open-source software, such as Label Studio and MLflow. We show that our annotation engine supports the further development of our in-house hierarchical classification systems, in particular, of scientific documents. Based on our previous work on hierarchical discipline classifications, we demonstrate SAINE's use for understanding the space for scholarly publications. The user study of our annotation results shows how the user input processed with SAINE can support a better understanding of the document classification process. SAINE can be particularly useful in fostering the transparency of meta-science research.

1 Introduction

A precise classification of publications across and within disciplines is key not only for a fast and comprehensive search to guide researchers to relevant material but also to identify the novelty of research, the standing and significance of scholars, and of the relative growth of fields of work (Bransford et al., 1999; Tsien, 2007; Kowsari et al., 2017; Frodeman et al., 2017; Semantic Scholar, 2022; Rao et al., 2023).

Machine learning develops into not only *a* but *the* customary approach to establish such a classification. Clearly, one would expect a search that is geared towards identifying a high-quality corpus of keywords to benefit crucially from supervision. Existing classifications of academic output, such as field of studies presented by Microsoft Academic Graphs (MAG) and OpenAlex (MAG successor), are based on a blend of (supervised) author-chosen and (unsupervised) machine-chosen keyword lists, where the composition of the blend is unknown to the researcher (Sinha et al., 2015; Shen et al., 2018; Wang et al., 2019a; Rao et al., 2023).

Prevailing systems, such as MAG, Dimensions, CrossRef, Web of Science (WoS), Scopus, or Google Scholar, provide keywords for academic publications, which are lists based on abstracts in a discipline, field, and subfield, distilled from unsupervised machine learning, from word or phrase frequencies; or supervised learning, mostly from keyword self-reporting by authors; or semi-supervised learning, a mixture of the two, e.g., as done by MAG described in Sinha et al. (2015); Wang et al. (2019b, 2020). As reported in Rao et al. (2023), the quality of keywords in MAG hinders the further development of meta-science projects as their quality vary from discipline to discipline, and the granularity forbids us to have an even comparison of research output across disciplines, fields, and disciplines. Hence, the motivation of this work is two-fold. On one hand, it is of interest to the meta-science community to understand the generation of these keywords and how they are associated with the classification of disciplines, fields, and subfields. On the other hand, it is crucial to understand the outputs of the model in the classification systems (Rao et al., 2023) that we develop and continuously improve.

For designing an annotation and inference engine that helps establishing a classification system of scientific publications, one would target developing a tool with the following features: (1) a simple user interface with clear annotation instructions; (2) a reproducible pipeline across various disciplines; (3) good support for inference tailored to downstream tasks (e.g., model retraining) in meta-science studies. To the best of our knowledge, SAINE is the first scientific annotation engine specifically targeted towards understanding the model output in terms of label assignments and keyword representation. Our tool is one of its own kind in annotating scientific documents, which allows us to qualitatively understand an ML model in classifying scientific works.[1]

[1]We provide here a brief literature review for scientific annotations. Early work on understanding scientific documents

Proceedings of the 13th International Joint Conference on Natural Language Processing and the 3rd Conference of the Asia-Pacific Chapter of the Association for Computational Linguistics: System Demonstrations, pages 41–58
November 1–4, 2023.

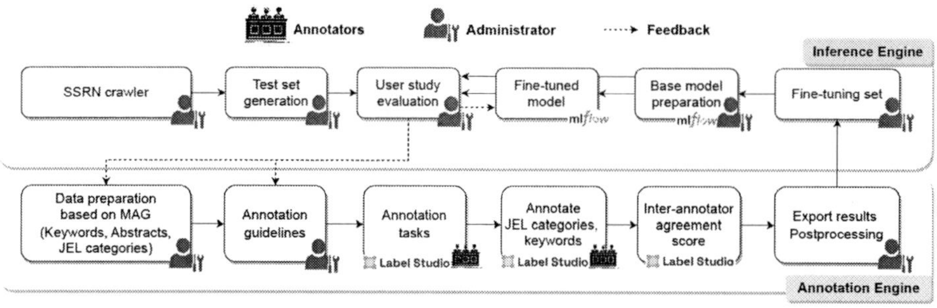

Figure 1: SAINE Workflow and Pipeline.

Among the existing open-source annotation tools, Label Studio (Tkachenko et al., 2020-2022) suits those needs. Note that Gayoso-Cabada et al. (2019) have reviewed extensively the annotation tools that facilitate classification tasks. However, the reviewed tools are either not open-sourced or are domain-specific and, hence, do not share the aforementioned targeted features.

In this system demonstration, we utilize a set of standard open-source software, mainly Label Studio (Tkachenko et al., 2020-2022), MLflow,[2] FastAPI,[3] and Pydantic[4] to configure an annotation and inference engine for scientific publication annotations. In this demonstration, we illustrate the benefit of using supervised learning based on pre-established keyword lists and abstracts, and how annotators can help us better understand the importance of *supervised* learning in establishing a classification of academic publications.

This system is built on top of the hitherto largest-scale *multi-class* hierarchical classification study across all academic research disciplines in both *single-label* and *multi-label* settings (cf. Rao et al. (2023)). There, we have built a supervised hierarchical classification system that associates every publication with at least one and potentially several disciplines, fields, and subfields.

With the annotations above, we conduct a small user study with domain experts using our **annotation** engine. We then invoke our **inference** engine to fine-tune the base models in Rao et al. (2023). The comparison between the base and fine-tuned models shows that the proposed annotation and inference system is able to benefit the development of more accurate classifications.

To summarize, the paper presents a scientific annotation and inference engine called SAINE, which is based on open-source software like Label Studio and MLflow. **The main contributions of the paper are:** (1) The demonstration of using SAINE in understanding the space for scholarly publications, particularly in hierarchical discipline classifications. (2) The result of a user study, which shows that user input collected with the help of SAINE can help better understand the classification process. (3) The ability of SAINE to benefit the further development of a more accurate classification, demonstrated through the comparison between the base and fine-tuned models. (4) The potential of SAINE to support downstream meta-science projects and foster greater transparency and understanding of scientific research.

The paper presents the benefits of supervised learning and the importance of a simple user interface with clear annotation instructions, reproducible pipelines, and good support for annotating and inferring scientific publications. The demonstration video can be accessed from `https://youtu.be/yToO-G9YQK4`. A live demo website is available at `https://app.heartex.com/user/signup/?token=e2435a2f97449fa1` upon free registration. The project codebase is available at https://gitlab.ethz.ch/raox/science-clf/-/tree/labelstudio and is merged with the codebase of Rao et al. (2023). We welcome collaboration

began with annotated segments of scientific articles for the purpose of information retrieval (Ibekwe-Sanjuan et al., 2011). Note that Gayoso-Cabada et al. (2019) have extensively reviewed the annotation tools that facilitate classification tasks. However, the reviewed tools are either not open-source or domain-specific, and hence do not share the aforementioned targeted features. Domain-specific efforts have been made to connect expert annotations and ontologies (Ciccarese et al., 2012). Ciccarese et al. (2011) discussed scientific document annotation as Resource Description Framework (RDF), which allows us to publish the annotation data as Linked Open Data, query it using languages such as SPARQL, and reason about it with SWRL. Small-scale studies (Zargayouna et al., 2016) have been conducted to annotate semantic roles in scientific articles. And knowledge graphs built on the topic of these annotations are studied (Luan et al., 2018; Zevio et al., 2020).

[2]`https://mlflow.org/`.

[3]`https://fastapi.tiangolo.com/`.

[4]`https://pydantic-docs.helpmanual.io/`.

and feedback from the scientific community.[5]

In Figure 1 we illustrate the **workflow** in SAINE by assigning the roles of "Administrator", "Annotators", "Label Studio", and "MLflow" to each task in the pipeline. With Label Studio we assign the annotation tasks to annotators and curators; MLflow was used to keep track of pre-trained models reported in Rao et al. (2023), which makes it easy to load a certain model for inspection and inference by simply specifying the experiment ID tracked using MLflow. We then build the inference engine with FastAPI and Pydantic: The former can be used to deploy machine learning models as web API services; the latter can be used to define data models for input and output data, which helps prevent errors and improves the reliability of the API.

The sections are organized as follows. Section 2 introduces the functionality of Label Studio and its fit to our annotation needs, as well as our annotation guidelines for experts. Section 3 specifies the annotation design for the field of *Economics* and discusses the annotation results. Section 4 discusses the integration of annotation results into the pre-trained base models and the fine-tuned ones with MLflow. We devote Section 5 to discuss our preliminary experiments on improving annotation efficiency. We then conclude this system demonstration with a discussion of future work, system limitations, ethics, and broader impact statements.

2 Annotating Scientific Articles with Label Studio

We briefly introduce functionalities of Label Studio and illustrate why Label Studio is a suitable tool to annotate scientific articles. **The goals of annotations in the present context are three: (1) [To judge the appropriateness of an assigned category.]** Experts judge whether a scientific article has a correctly assigned category. If a category does not suit the abstract's content, the annotator will pick a new category from a pre-defined list. **(2) [To evaluate keywords.]** Experts evaluate keywords assigned by Microsoft Academic Graph (MAG) and mark missing keywords in the abstract. **(3) [To calculate inter-annotator agreement.]** The annotation engine should permit an efficient way of calculating inter-annotator agreement (IAA) scores among annotators.

[5]Note that the annotation engine is used for internal testing at the moment but will open for beta testing for all disciplines soon. We have over 100 users queuing for the beta stage. We are working on incorporating user profiles through self-declaration or automatic screening. The results of the beta stage will be shared with the community in due course.

2.1 Label Studio

Label Studio is a powerful and versatile annotation tool that can handle various types of annotation tasks. Here are some of the features of Label Studio that make it suitable for the annotation tasks.

- **[Customizable interface.]** Label Studio allows us to design a customized annotation interface. One can create a pre-defined list of categories for the experts to choose from and provide them with clear instructions on how to evaluate the assigned category.
- **[Multiple annotation types.]** Label Studio supports various types of annotation, including text classification, entity recognition, and sequence labeling. Therefore, different types of annotation can be used to evaluate keywords, mark missing keywords, and judge predicted categories.
- **[Collaboration and version control.]** Label Studio enables multiple experts to work on the same project simultaneously, allowing efficient and collaborative annotation. It also includes a version control system that tracks changes to the annotations, facilitating easy comparison and IAA evaluation.
- **[Inter-annotator agreement (IAA).]** Label Studio has built-in tools to calculate IAA scores. These tools can help evaluate the consistency and reliability of chosen annotations.
- **[Integrations with machine-learning models.]** Label Studio also provides integration with various machine learning (ML) models. Although we do not use the integrated ML functions, Label Studio allows us to export the annotation results in JSON, with which we improve the classification models using the annotated data in the inference engine.

Overall, Label Studio offers a powerful and customizable annotation platform that can handle relevant annotation tasks, facilitate efficient collaboration among experts, and efficiently compute IAA.

The project manager uses an administrative panel (Figure 4 in Appendix B) to assign annotation tasks to each registered annotator and can monitor the annotation progress. The manager can also adjust the assigned annotations based on individual progress, as well as inspect tasks by annotation progress and IAA metrics.

2.2 Annotation Guidelines

When a publication is annotated, each annotator is provided with the abstract, the keywords offered by MAG, and the assigned category based on the keywords provided by MAG. The categories of a discipline classification (such as the Journal of Economic Literature, JEL, clasification in economics) are assigned to MAG publications on the basis of the keywords. Therefore, MAG's keywords help us identify potential misalignments and better understand the classifiers we built.

The annotation samples provided in the annotation engine are stratified sampled (ratio: 2e-5) across all classes of the training set introduced by Rao et al. (2023) for one discipline. Each annotator is required to judge whether a category is correctly assigned to an abstract. If not, the annotator is required to select the suitable one from a predefined list. The annotator is also required to evaluate MAG-generated keywords and make corrections (by removing unqualified keywords/marking suitable keywords from the abstract). Figure 2 shows two annotations of one publication. Label Studio makes it easy to navigate among the annotations generated by various annotators on an identical instance. Note that, as we discussed in Rao et al. (2023), our multi-class hierarchical classification system is modularized in both *single-label* and *multi-label* settings.[6] The current annotation engine is equipped with both annotation functionalities. For the sake of system demonstration and user study in Section 3, we discuss the *single-label* setting. More details on the multi-label setting are provided in Appendix C.

3 Implementation: User Study in *Economics*

We now use *Economics* as a discipline to show how we utilize the annotation engine to collect expert annotations.

3.1 Annotation Design

We invited three economist experts from the Chair of Applied Economics at ETH Zurich to join the annotation project by accessing this link.[7] Annotation guidelines are given at our project repository.[8] Of the three experts, one has annotated all provided instances (Annotator 1), one has annotated 10% of the instances (Annotator 2), and one has annotated a subset of instances with an *ex ante* denomination in Urban and Spatial Economics only (Annotator 3). Each annotator received a user panel like Figure 5 in Appendix B.

3.2 Annotation Results in Label Studio

Altogether, 788 instances of abstracts and keywords from MAG had to be annotated for a *single-label* classification. In Economics, a standardized field and subfield system with keywords exists, and it is called the Journal of Economic Literature (JEL) classification system.[9] This system is known to all academic economists and serves as a guiding principle to associate an article or a topic with a specific subfield in *Economics*. The subfields in the JEL categories are associated with keywords.

We report the annotation time and IAA scores across all tasks that are automatically calculated by Label Studio.[10] The final task agreement score is calculated by averaging all IAA scores for each annotation pair. Table 1 illustrates the IAA scores amongst three experts. Annotators 1, 2, and 3 have annotated 788, 181, and 99 instances, respectively. The number of overlapping tasks between annotator pairs is 52 (Annotators 2 and 3), 99 (Annotators 1 and 3), and 181 (Annotators 1 and 2), respectively. The median annotation time of Annotators 1-3 per instance was 17.7s, 29.8s, and 40.9s, respectively. The annotators were entitled to disapprove of the assigned category based on MAG upon suggesting an alternative category. Marking and filling in missing keywords is time consuming, and reading the MAG-generated keywords can help, to some extent, the annotation speed. However, all annotators reported that MAG-provided keywords could be a source of error for incorrectly assigned categories. As discussed among the annotators after they underwent the annotations separately, the category they found the best was for *Mathematical & Quantitative Methods*, and it was worst for *Macroeconomics* and *Public Economics*.[11]

[6] We offer an brief overview of our hierarchical classification system in Appendix A.

[7] https://app.heartex.com/user/signup/?token=edd1c85b0a9c9cd2.

[8] https://gitlab.ethz.ch/raox/science-clf/-/blob/labelstudio/labelstudio/annotation_guideline.md.

[9] https://www.aeaweb.org/econlit/jelCodes.php?view=jel.

[10] See the official documentation under this link (https://labelstud.io/guide/stats.html) for the IAA calculation steps. Using the "Basic matching function" gives us the current results in Table 1 while using the "exact matching" gives us even better results.

[11] We are aware that we need to assign budget to incentive potential expert annotators. In collaboration with Open

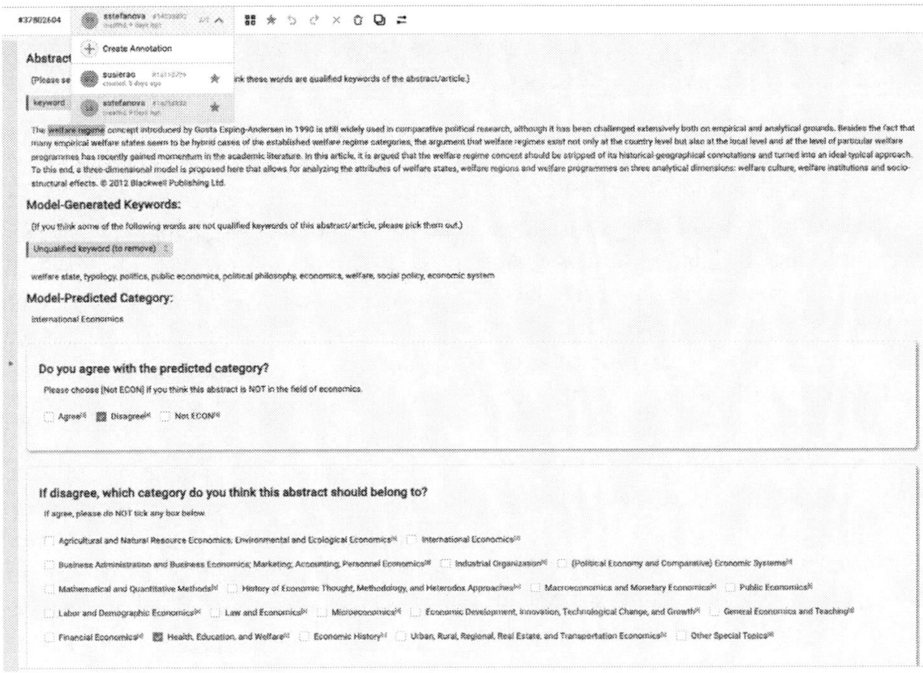

Figure 2: Publication Annotations by Multiple Annotators.

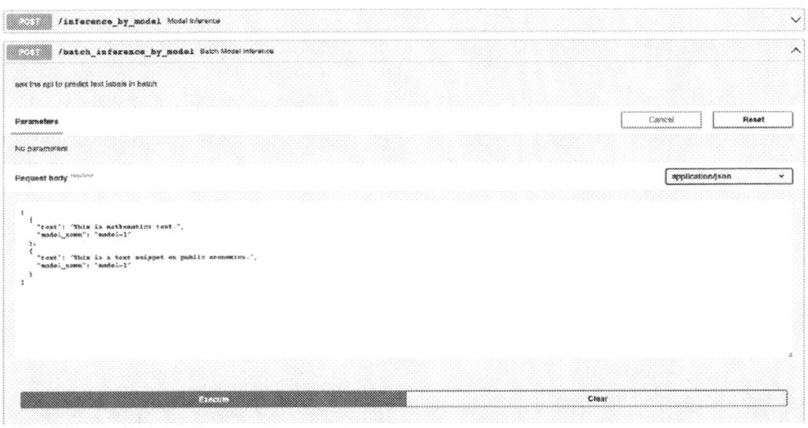

Figure 3: Inference Engine with *MLflow* Integration. API: Batch Inference by Model.

	Annotator 1	Annotator 2	Annotator 3
Annotator 1		55%	55%
Annotator 2	55%		27%
Annotator 3	55%	27%	

Table 1: Annotator Agreement Matrix Among Three Expert Annotators.

4 Inference Engine: Incorporating Annotation Results into the Existing Classification Pipeline

We illustrate the pipeline using the discipline of *Economics* as discussed in Section 3.

Research Data Call (https://ethrat.ch/en/eth-domain/open-research-data/) and ETH Library, we are exploring possible ways to remunerate high-quality annotations.

4.1 Post-processing of Annotation Results

We downloaded the annotation results in JSON[12] of all experts and post-processed them following the protocols below, before feeding them into the pre-trained base models of various neural networks as discussed in Rao et al. (2023). In total, we obtained 1,068 partly overlapping annotations (incl. "Skip", "(Dis)agree", keywords, added categories). The basic statistics on the number of instances of "Agree", "Disagree" and "Not ECON" are 498, 297, and 268,

[12]The annotation results are accessible under https://gitlab.ethz.ch/raox/science-clf/-/blob/labelstudio/labelstudio/labeled_data/labelstudio_econ.json.

respectively.

The post-processing procedure is structured as follows. (1) We removed abstracts that were inadequately classified as belonging in *Economics* from the sample (206 of 788 instances). Additionally, we deleted 5 instances due to bad annotations. For example, no one labeled this sample ("Skip"), or an annotator chose "Disagree" but did not choose a new category. (2) For each remaining instance, we counted the percentages of *"Agree"* and *"Disagree"* verdicts relative to the label generated on the basis of MAG keywords. If strictly more experts agreed than disagreed with MAG, the original label was preserved (for 351 of the 577 valid instances). Otherwise, we took the label suggested by the majority of annotating experts (for 226 of the 577 valid instances). (3) In the case of ties, we randomly picked a label from the suggested annotations (for 22 of the 226 category-renewed instances). Following this protocol, we obtained 561 instances with expert-curated labels to fine-tune the base models.

4.2 Fine-tuning Pre-trained Base Models

We used the 561 labels generated by the experts as a fine-tuning set on the base models reported in Rao et al. (2023) on the discipline of *Economics* (model-1). We compared the inference performances of the base model (**Model** in Table 2) with those of the fine-tuned model (**Model_FT** in Table 2) on various neural network architectures, Deep Neural Network (DNN), Recurrent Neural Network (RNN), Convolutional Neural Network (CNN), and Transformers. To benchmark the differences in performances between **Model** and **Model_FT**, we created a small test set from the Social Science Research Network (SSRN),[13] which is a website that provides a platform for researchers to share and distribute their research papers and other scholarly work in the social sciences and other related fields. We decided to use the *Economics* SSRN publications because they come with human-currated JEL categories, keywords, and abstracts.

Concretely, we built an SSRN crawler[14] to download the publication space in Economics publications in SSRN, where all contained research articles in Economics are multi-category-indexed. This means, each publication there is indexed by at least one JEL code and it allows multiple JEL codes per publication. We could easily validate with our multi-label engine in principal, but we focus on *single-label* classifications for this user study.

Model (1)	Model_FT (2)	Δ(Model_FT−Model) (3)	Model = Model_FT (4)	Total (5)	Model Type (6)
54	58	4	108		CNN
59	69	10	148	190	**RNN**
39	39	0	190		DNN
31	33	2	37		Transformer

Table 2: Results of the User Study. *FT*: Fine-tuned.

To create this test set, we randomly sampled 10 instances from each of 19 JEL field classes, which resulted in a sample of 190 test instances. In the implementation of hierarchical classifications reported in Rao et al. (2023), we have used MLflow to track and manage ML experiments, with which we have saved all pre-trained base models. Now, based on them, we could seamlessly integrate model fine-tuning and inference with various models. The inference engine API has been implemented using FastAPI with help from Pydantic.[15] We illustrate the batch inference API in Figure 3, with which users can feed the test set into various models (base or fine-tuned) and obtain predictions. In Appendix D we provide more details about the inference engine.

4.3 Benefits of Expert Annotations

We present the results of user studies in Table 2. Specifically, we inspect two types of statistics, the correct predictions of the base and fine-tuned models in Columns (1)-(2), and the identical predictions of the base and fine-tuned models in Column (4). Since each publication is multi-JEL-category-indexed, we count the prediction as "correct" if the indices include the predicted category. Column (1) is the base model trained with the model type specified in Column (6). Column (2) presents the results of the fine-tuned (supervised) model. Column (4) shows that out of a total of 190 test instances, identical predictions were generated by the base and fine-tuned models. We see that fine-tuning with user-generated results has brought benefits to all

[13]The test set is accessible under `https://www.ssrn.com/index.cfm/en/`.

[14]Our crawler is accessible under `https://gitlab.ethz.ch/raox/science-clf/-/tree/labelstudio/labelstudio/ssrn_crawler` and the publications on economics on SSRN can be retrieved under `https://papers.ssrn.com/sol3/displayjel.cfm`.

[15]FastAPI (`https://fastapi.tiangolo.com/`) and Pydantic (`https://pydantic-docs.helpmanual.io/`) are two Python libraries commonly used in machine learning and web development to build robust and efficient APIs. Combining them allows us to create APIs with strong data validation, asynchronous support for handling multiple requests, and automatic documentation generation. This combination simplifies the deployment of machine learning models as web services while maintaining code quality and reliability.

models except DNN because DNN predicts for all test examples only one class (the dominating one). RNN is the best performer when considering the benefits resulting from expert supervision, because the Δ in correct predictions has increased the most according to Column (3). Interestingly, fine-tuning a pre-trained Transformer model may not always result in a significant improvement in performance, as we see from a comparison with other base models. However, the current fine-tuning set is too small to draw firm conclusions in this regard.

5 Discussions: Improving Annotation Efficiency

We share preliminary results of improving annotation efficiency based on the annotators' feedback.

5.1 Similarity between Articles and Scholars

First, we assume that we have access to the annotators' Google Scholar profiles and their self-reported fields of expertise.[16] Then we assume that these two sets of labels do not vary largely, which gives us a high confidence score about one annotator. Finally, we match the best-suited scholars to the articles to annotate by extracting keywords from the top-cited articles of these scholars and scoring them on the cosine similarity with the article keywords. The results are promising and can reduce work overhead for the scholars while improving the quality of the annotations by assigning best suited scholars for the process. More details on the implementation are given in Appendix E.

5.2 LLM as Annotators

Do we still need the supervised learning models now that we have the mighty LLM models? How well do LLMs perform these annotation tasks? In light of our commitment to total project transparency, we have opted to utilize the Vicuna 7B and 13B models (Chiang et al., 2023), both of which are publicly available for non-commercial use and are fine-tuned based on LLaMA (Touvron et al., 2023), explicitly tailored for QA tasks. For their predictions on single-label and multi-label classifications, see Tables 3 and 4. Overall, we observe that even one of the best LLMs performs poorly in the *single-label* setting and has potential to be used as keyword extractor and annotate *multi-label* classifications. The details of the experimental protocols are in Appendix F.

[16]Each annotator will be asked to fill in a self-declaration form (https://gitlab.ethz.ch/raox/science-clf/-/blob/labelstudio/labelstudio/Scholar%20Similarity/Researcher_Details.pdf) before we assign the annotator's tasks.

Vicuna	Agree	Disagree	NOT ECON	Blank	Total
7B	740	28	16	4	788
13B	122	648	7	11	788

Table 3: Results of *Single-Label* Prediction by Vicuna. Those Vicuna outputs that do not contain the keywords "Agree", "Disagree" or "NOT ECON" are labeled as "blank".

Vicuna	ECON (Y/N)	Cat1 (A/D/B)	Cat2 (A/D/B)	Cat3 (A/D/B)
7B	417 / 297	157 / 146 / 114	122 / 199 / 96	5 / 18 / 10
13B	614 / 100	158 / 445 / 11	121 / 490 / 3	3 / 39 / 0

Table 4: Results of *Multi-Label* Prediction by Vicuna. Y/N - "Yes"/"No", A/D/B - "Agree"/"Disagree"/"Blank". "Cat1,2,3" are three predicted labels by our classification system. If it predicts that an abstract does not belong to ECON, then we will no longer ask whether or not it agrees with the our model-predicted categories. Responses that do not contain the specified keywords are considered "blank". The dataset contains a total of 42 entries with non-empty Cat3. In this subset, Vicuna-13B uniformly classifies all entries to be in the ECON domain. Conversely, Vicuna-7B predicts 33 of these entries within the ECON domain.

6 Conclusions and Future Work

In this system demonstration, we utilize a set of standard open-source software, mainly Label Studio (Tkachenko et al., 2020-2022), MLflow, FastAPI and Pydantic, to configure an annotation and inference engine for scientific publications (SAINE). This system is built on top of hitherto largest multi-class hierarchical classification study across all disciplines in both single-label and multi-label settings (cf. Rao et al. (2023)). We illustrate the functionality of the system with a user study in *Economics* and show that expert inputs to our system can help better understand the classification process, which benefits the development of a stronger model in the next iteration. We plan to open-source the data and codebase and invite collaborative work in the direction of meta-science. SAINE can bring about societal and scholarly impact in enabling more transparent and rigorous scientific research understanding by promoting ethical AI usage and responsible research practices.

In future work, we plan to expand SAINE to include different scientific disciplines, which allows us to conduct larger-scale user studies; we also plan to explore *multi-label* annotation tasks in all levels including disciplines, fields and subfields. As already discussed in Section 5, we plan to leverage LLMs to assist in annotations, as well as to automatically select the suitable annotators based on their profiles and publications to annotate.

Limitations

Label Studio has some limitations in incorporating existing ML pipelines into the annotation engine, especially, when using customary code. It is not clear from the documentation (https://labelstud.io/guide/ml.html) how to deploy the ML backend with pre-trained models. We will discuss this with the developers at Label Studio and see how we can bring the annotation engine and the ML pipeline closer to each other.

In terms of annotator selection, at the moment we have to select the experts for each discipline. However, we have performed experiments to rank annotators according to their field expertise and find the best annotation tasks based on the similarity between the space for academic publications and the space for articles (Appendix E). One future idea is to automatically compute an associative score between a third-party academic product such as Google Scholar and the publication space. For instance, the project PeopleMap[17] provides interesting techniques to generate researcher profiles based on their research interests and publications taking as input the URLs of the researchers' Google Scholar profile. At this stage, Label Studio developers suggest that we add a self-declarative questionnaire to each annotator, which can be used as meta-data on annotators when quantifying the annotation confidence score. Due to time constraints, we have not yet added this questionnaire in the user study reported in the current manuscript, as the experts in the current user study are selected by our project PI and have strong expertise in *Economics*. However, we will incorporate this self-declaration questionnaire in the beta testing stage.

In terms of annotation efforts, we have benchmarked annotation quality using LLMs, which shows that human annotators are needed to control the quality. Considering our annotators' feedback that it is time-consuming to extract keywords for humans, it makes sense to use LLMs as an annotation-assisting engine for keyword extraction at this stage. We have evaluated the LLM-generated keywords: some are quite generic given the context, and others are good fits. We plan to do a systematic evaluation of LLM-generated keywords using the WOS-46985 benchmark dataset.[18] In terms of label prediction, we see in Tables 3 and 4 that Vicuna performs poorly on the *single-label* task and we will need to finish a larger sample of *multi-label* task to gauge its values, despite its superior performances in 100 tasks we evaluate against human performance.

Ethics Statement

We acknowledge that our system may involve processing potentially sensitive data (such as annotator profile), and we take data privacy and ethical considerations very seriously. In accordance with ethical guidelines of "ACM Code of Ethics", we will take steps to protect the privacy of annotators once the annotation engine is in the beta stage. Only annotation administrators have access to the results of researcher questionnaires. On the Label Studio platform (see https://labelstud.io/blog/human-feedback-in-ai/), the annotators' tasks and profiles are unknown to their peers. We also enable a comparison between subjective evaluation (by self-declaration) and objective evaluation (by past publication records of the annotators) to mitigate biases. We have also made efforts to ensure that our system and its annotations are unbiased and fair. We believe that our work will help foster greater transparency and understanding in scientific research, and we welcome collaboration and feedback from the scientific community to further advance ethical and responsible use of AI in research.

Broader Impact Statement

Our annotation engine and inference engine can further support downstream meta-science projects. We list a few interesting questions we can answer using our pipeline (Rao et al. (2023) and the annotation and inference engine).

1. **[For students.]** Which fields of research are more impactful/growing?
2. **[For policy makers.]** How to design education for cross-/inter-/pluridisciplinary studies?
3. **[For department and tenure committees.]** How to benchmark output and impact levels of an untenured scholar?
4. **[For funding institutions.]** How to measure/quantify inter-/pluri-disciplinary standards for institutions such as SNIS and SNSF that emphasize the interdisciplinarity of research?[19]

[17] https://github.com/poloclub/people-map.

[18] https://paperswithcode.com/sota/document-classification-on-wos-46985.

[19] SNIS: https://snis.ch/, SNSF: https://www.snf.ch/en.

5. **[For librarians.]** How can one effectively organize bibliographical resources across disciplines and departments in one university?[20]

We plan to add other disciplines covered by Rao et al. (2023) to our annotation engine. We would also like to incorporate subjective (self-declaration) and objective measurements (e.g., Google Scholar profile integration) into the annotation pipeline. This may help develop confidence scores of one annotation/annotator.

Acknowledgements

We thank the colleagues at DS3Lab (https://ds3lab.inf.ethz.ch/) for providing valuable feedback when prototyping the system design. Without the strong support of our expert group at the Chair of Applied Economics (https://cae.ethz.ch/), the user study would not have been possible. We thank Mr. Prakhar Bhandari and Ms. Piriyakorn Piriyatamwong for their technical support to our project. We appreciate that Label Studio has offered us an academic license for the project, which allows us to invite more experts to contribute in the long run. The user agreement and terms of an academic license are listed https://labelstud.io/academic/.

References

John D Bransford, Ann L Brown, and Rodney R Cocking. 1999. How people learn: Brain, mind, experience, and school. *Washington, DC: National Academy Press. ED*, 436:276.

Marco Campos. 2020. Yake: Yet another keyword extractor. https://github.com/LIAAD/yake.

Sahil Chaddha. 2020. Python implementation of rapid automatic keyword extraction using nltk. https://csurfer.github.io/rake-nltk/_build/html/index.html.

Wei-Lin Chiang, Zhuohan Li, Zi Lin, Ying Sheng, Zhanghao Wu, Hao Zhang, Lianmin Zheng, Siyuan Zhuang, Yonghao Zhuang, Joseph E. Gonzalez, Ion Stoica, and Eric P. Xing. 2023. Vicuna: An open-source chatbot impressing gpt-4 with 90%* chatgpt quality.

Paolo Ciccarese, Marco Ocana, and Tim Clark. 2012. Open semantic annotation of scientific publications using DOMEO. In *Journal of Biomedical Semantics*, volume 3, pages 1–14. BioMed Central.

[20] Our team is invited to contribute to a blog post of Swiss Year of Scientometrics (https://yearofscientometrics.ethz.ch/), a project of ETH Library, funded by swissuniversities (https://www.swissuniversities.ch/en/).

Paolo Ciccarese, Marco Ocana, Leyla Jael Garcia Castro, Sudeshna Das, and Tim Clark. 2011. An open annotation ontology for science on Web 3.0. In *Journal of Biomedical Semantics*, volume 2, pages 1–24. BioMed Central.

Robert Frodeman, Julie Thompson Klein, and Roberto Carlos Dos Santos Pacheco. 2017. *The Oxford Handbook of Interdisciplinarity*. Oxford University Press.

Joaquín Gayoso-Cabada, Antonio Sarasa-Cabezuelo, and José-Luis Sierra-Rodríguez. 2019. A review of annotation classification tools in the educational domain. *Open Computer Science*, 9(1):299–307.

Maarten Grootendorst. 2020. Keybert: Minimal keyword extraction with bert.

Fidelia Ibekwe-Sanjuan, Fernandez Silvia, Sanjuan Eric, and Charton Eric. 2011. Annotation of scientific summaries for information retrieval. *arXiv preprint arXiv:1110.5722*.

Kamran Kowsari, Donald E Brown, Mojtaba Heidarysafa, Kiana Jafari Meimandi, Matthew S Gerber, and Laura E Barnes. 2017. HDLTex: Hierarchical deep learning for text classification. In *2017 16th IEEE International Conference on Machine Learning and Applications (ICMLA)*, pages 364–371. IEEE.

Yi Luan, Luheng He, Mari Ostendorf, and Hannaneh Hajishirzi. 2018. Multi-task identification of entities, relations, and coreference for scientific knowledge graph construction. *arXiv preprint arXiv:1808.09602*.

OpenAI. 2023. Gpt-4 technical report.

Susie Xi Rao, Peter H Egger, and Ce Zhang. 2023. Hierarchical classification of research fields in the "web of science" using deep learning. *arXiv preprint arXiv:2302.00390*.

Susie Xi Rao, Piriyakorn Piriyatamwong, Parijat Ghoshal, Sara Nasirian, Emmanuel de Salis, Sandra Mitrović, Michael Wechner, Vanya Brucker, Peter Egger, and Ce Zhang. 2022. Keyword extraction in scientific documents. *arXiv preprint arXiv:2207.01888*.

Semantic Scholar. 2022. Announcing s2fos, an open source academic field of study classifier. *AI2 Blog*. [Online; accessed: 2022-11-22].

Zhihong Shen, Hao Ma, and Kuansan Wang. 2018. A web-scale system for scientific knowledge exploration. *arXiv preprint arXiv:1805.12216*.

Arnab Sinha, Zhihong Shen, Yang Song, Hao Ma, Darrin Eide, Bo-june Paul Hsu, and Kuansan Wang. 2015. An overview of microsoft academic service (MAS) and applications. In *Proceedings of the 24th international conference on world wide web*, pages 243–246. ACM.

Maxim Tkachenko, Mikhail Malyuk, Andrey Holmanyuk, and Nikolai Liubimov. 2020-2022. Label Studio: Data labeling software. Open source software available from https://github.com/heartexlabs/label-studio.

TogetherComputer. 2023. OpenChatKit: An Open Toolkit and Base Model for Dialogue-style Applications.

Hugo Touvron, Thibaut Lavril, Gautier Izacard, Xavier Martinet, Marie-Anne Lachaux, Timothée Lacroix, Baptiste Rozière, Naman Goyal, Eric Hambro, Faisal Azhar, Aurelien Rodriguez, Armand Joulin, Edouard Grave, and Guillaume Lample. 2023. Llama: Open and efficient foundation language models.

Joe Z Tsien. 2007. The memory code. *Scientific American*, 297(1):52–59.

Kuansan Wang, Zhihong Shen, Chiyuan Huang, Chieh-Han Wu, Yuxiao Dong, and Anshul Kanakia. 2020. Microsoft academic graph: When experts are not enough. *Quantitative Science Studies*, 1(1):396–413.

Kuansan Wang, Zhihong Shen, Chiyuan Huang, Chieh-Han Wu, Darrin Eide, Yuxiao Dong, Junjie Qian, Anshul Kanakia, Alvin Chen, and Richard Rogahn. 2019a. A review of Microsoft Academic Services for science of science studies. *Frontiers in Big Data*, 2:45.

Kuansan Wang, Zhihong Shen, Chiyuan Huang, Chieh-Han Wu, Darrin Eide, Yuxiao Dong, Junjie Qian, Anshul Kanakia, Alvin Chen, and Richard Rogahn. 2019b. A review of microsoft academic services for science of science studies. *Frontiers in Big Data*, 2.

Haïfa Zargayouna, Davide Buscaldi, Isabelle Tellier, and Thierry Charnois. 2016. Semantic annotation of the ACL anthology corpus for the automatic analysis of scientific literature. In *LREC 2016*.

Stella Zevio, Guillaume Santini, Henry Soldano, Haïfa Zargayouna, and Thierry Charnois. 2020. A combination of semantic annotation and graph mining for expert finding in scholarly data. In *Proceedings of the Graph Embedding and Mining (GEM) Workshop at ECML PKDD*.

Lianmin Zheng, Wei-Lin Chiang, Ying Sheng, Siyuan Zhuang, Zhanghao Wu, Yonghao Zhuang, Zi Lin, Zhuohan Li, Dacheng Li, Eric. P Xing, Hao Zhang, Joseph E. Gonzalez, and Ion Stoica. 2023. Judging llm-as-a-judge with mt-bench and chatbot arena.

A Our Hierarchical Classification System

We provide an overview of Rao et al. (2023). The presented paper introduces a modularized three-level hierarchical classification system designed to automatically categorize scholarly publications based on their abstracts. The system operates within a hierarchical label set consisting of disciplines, fields, and subfields, enabling multi-class classification. This approach facilitates a systematic categorization of research activities, considering both knowledge production and impact through citations. The system distinguishes 44 disciplines, 718 fields, and 1,485 subfields, leveraging a vast collection of abstract snippets from the Microsoft Academic Graph. By utilizing various neural network models, such as DNNs, RNNs (using GRU), CNNs, and Transformers, through batch training, the system achieves high classification accuracy rates exceeding 90% in both single-label and multi-label settings.

The modular design of the system allows for flexibility and easy integration of new models, with CNNs identified as the most efficient performer across the models. The system consists of three components: the first component (L1) handles discipline classification, the second component (L2) focuses on field classification, and the third component (L3) specializes in subfield classification. Each component operates based on the output of the previous level, enabling a granular categorization of research activities and capturing the interdisciplinary nature of certain topics.

In the classification process, the system assigns publications to disciplines, fields, and subfields based on their abstracts. It computes conditional probabilities to determine the relevance of each label given the previous level labels. This hierarchical approach improves the alignment of research texts with disciplines, enables automated classification, and captures interdisciplinarity.

The system incorporates both single-label and multi-label settings. In the single-label setting, each publication is assigned to a single category, while in the multi-label setting, publications can be assigned to multiple categories simultaneously. The multi-label classification assumes label independence and employs binary cross-entropy loss for training. To ensure a balanced distribution of relevant and irrelevant samples, stratified sampling is maintained for label sets.

Performance evaluation of the classification system includes metrics such as categorical accuracy, precision, and recall. The system's ability to accurately classify research texts, align them with relevant disciplines, and capture interdisciplinarity contributes to its value in indexing and analyzing scientific publications.

Overall, the proposed system, with its modular design and pretrained models, serves as a solid foundation for future applications in scientific publication indexing and analysis.

B Label Studio Functionalities

In Figure 4 we demonstrate the administrative panel of the project manager. The "Filters" and "Order (Annotation results)" tabs make it easy to inspect tasks by annotation progress (e.g., "Annotators", "Agreement", "Completed", "Total annotations per task"). In Figure 5, we demonstrate the user panel that we show for each expert annotator. Each annotator has no access to additional information about the annotations made by the other annotators. As an expert, one can only see how many annotations have been gathered per instance among the experts together.

C Multi-label Annotation Engine

The setup of multi-label annotation is similar to the single-label setting. In the multi-label settings, annotators are required to mark "(Dis)agree" for each suggested JEL category (we provide three categories at most) and then select additional JEL categories, where multiple choices are allowed.

D Inference Engine

We provide two types of API calls for inference, (1) `inference_by_model` and (2) `batch_inference_by_model`. The only difference between these two API calls is that API (2) allows text-label predictions in batches, which requires a JSON sequence as input. Figure 7 demonstrates the user interface.

E Similarity between Authors and Articles

E.1 Keyword Extraction

The process of keyword extraction from the top 25 cited articles of each author and individual publication articles involves the following steps and methods. The scholars we picked are five renowned economists and use Google Scholar to download their profiles and publications. We start with the abstracts from these articles as the primary source of information.

Firstly, we perform an initial cleaning and preprocessing on these abstracts. This cleaning involves the removal of non-alphanumeric characters, conversion of text to lowercase, and tokenization of the text into individual words. We also remove common words, known as stop words, which do not contribute much to the overall meaning of the text. Finally, we discard words that are less than three characters long as these are typically not meaningful. This cleaning process results in a simplified and standardized version of the original text which is more suitable for further analysis.

Secondly, we ensure that all our data is in English to maintain consistency. For this, we employ a language detection function. If a text is not in English, we translate it using a translation pipeline, which is a model capable of accurately translating text from various languages to English. To handle potential memory issues with larger texts, we split the text into smaller chunks, translate each chunk separately, and then concatenate them back together.

The cleaned and translated text is then passed through KeyBERT (Grootendorst, 2020), a minimalistic transformer-based keyphrase extraction technique, which is used to extract keywords from the text. Apart from KeyBERT we also tried other keyword extraction techniques like YAKE (Campos, 2020) and RAKE (Chaddha, 2020). We then compared which of these techniques extracted the best keywords by generating scores for the tasks on the benchmark data set "WOS-46985" discussed in (Rao et al., 2022). We found that KeyBERT got the best scores for the extracted keywords when compared to the reference data. KeyBERT uses BERT, a state-of-the-art transformer model for natural language processing, to convert words into high-dimensional vectors or embeddings. These embeddings capture the semantic meaning of the words and their context. KeyBERT then identifies clusters in these embeddings to find the most representative or "key" phrases.

We extract 250 keywords for each author by combining and analyzing the abstracts of their top 25 cited articles, which gives us a broad representation of their research interests. For individual publication articles, we extract 15 keywords to capture the essence of each specific article. We have tried 5, 10, 15 keywords for each article, and 15 gives the best results.

By following this methodology, we ensure the extraction of the most relevant and informative keywords for each author and individual article, providing us with a valuable understanding of the research

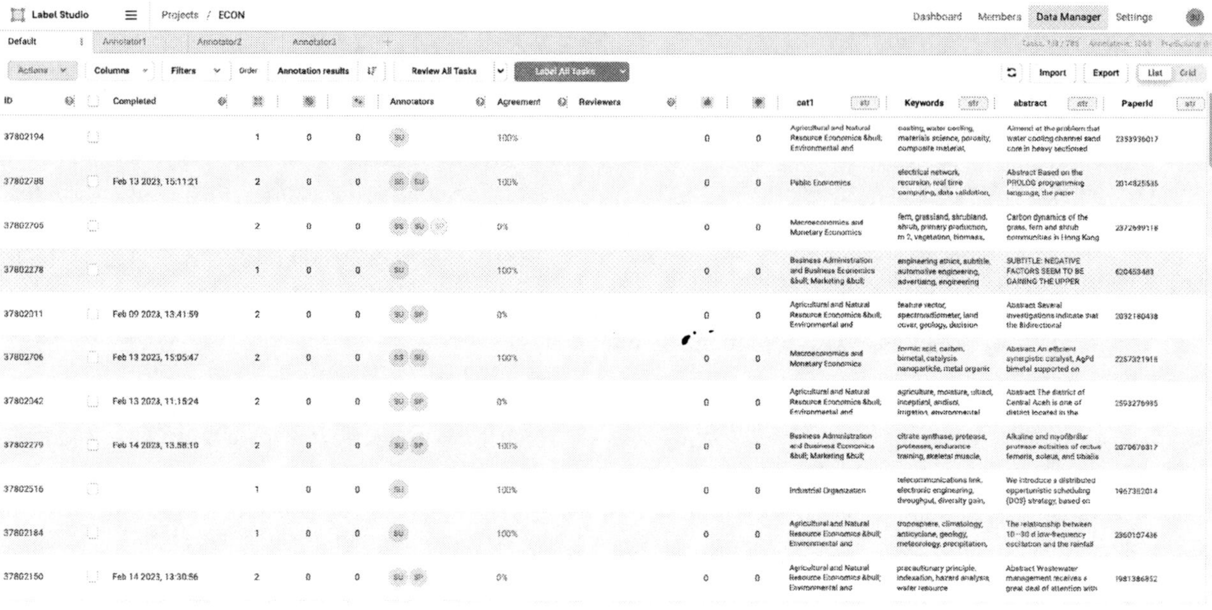

Figure 4: Administrative Panel of Annotation Tasks in Label Studio.

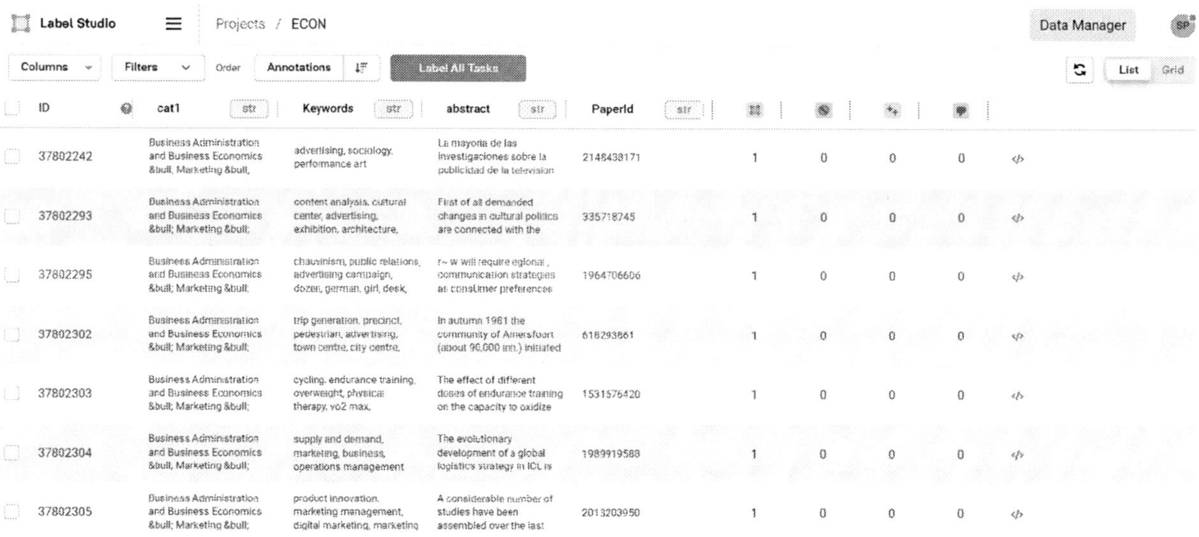

Figure 5: Annotator Panel of the Assigned Annotation Tasks in Label Studio.

landscape and the interests of the authors.

E.2 Similarity Scores

In our work, we present an innovative method that allows for a comprehensive understanding of the relationship between authors, publications, and research categories. This approach uses a function which not only identifies the top authors relevant to a particular article but also uncovers the top fields of research or "categories" connected to the article and hence its best annotator(s).

The function employs the TF-IDF (Term Frequency-Inverse Document Frequency) vectorization technique to transform text data into a numerical representation that can be processed by machine learning algorithms. For a given publication, it uses this technique to compare the article's abstract to those of top-cited authors, generating a list of the most similar authors.

Subsequently, the function identifies the top research categories linked to the publication by analyzing the keywords in its abstract. It applies the same process to the top-ranked author's 25 most cited articles. The result is a set of top categories that best align with the publication and the most relevant author, providing a deeper understanding

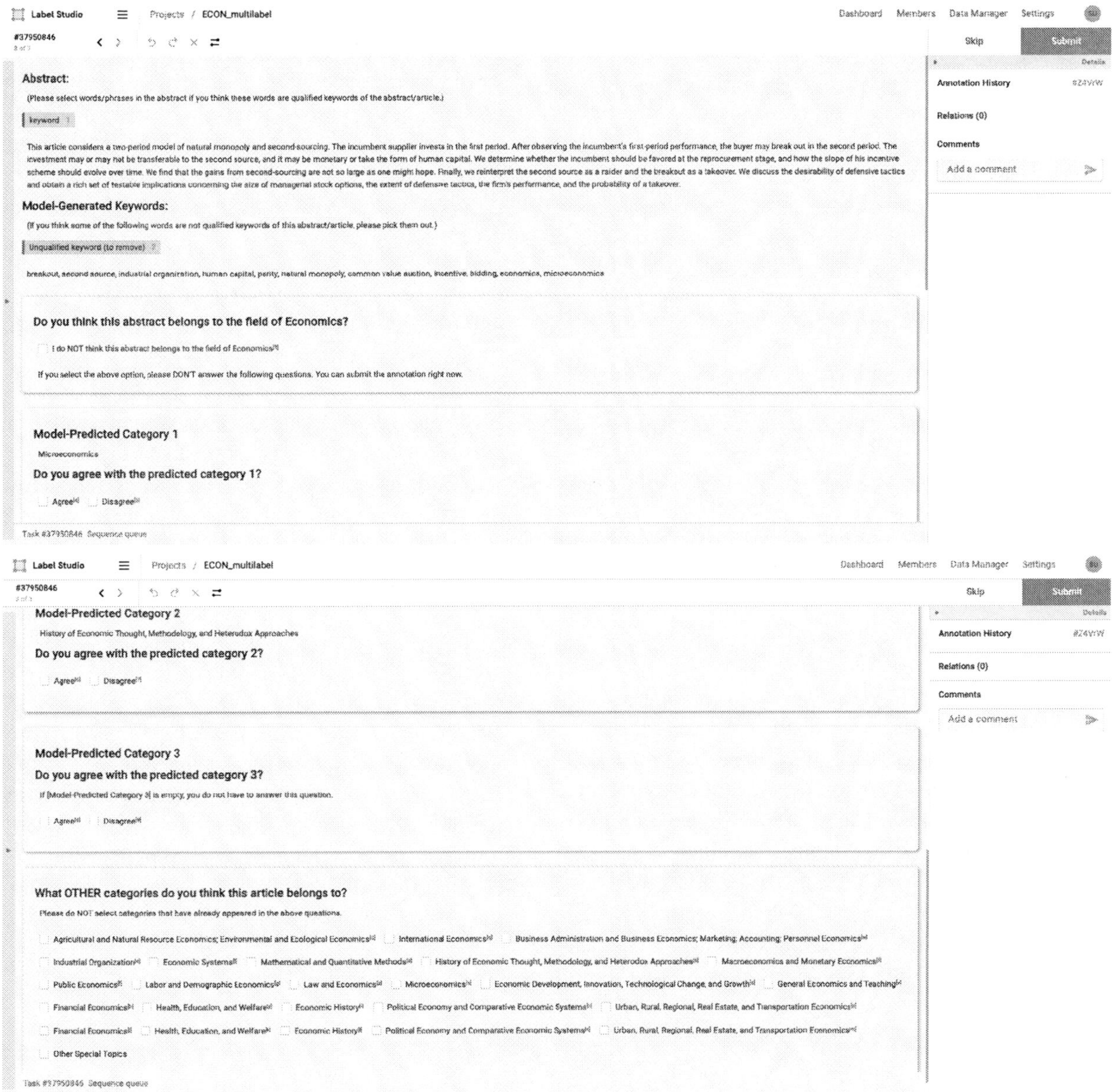

Figure 6: Publication Annotation Engine in a Multi-label Setting.

of their research focus. This novel approach offers a multidimensional view of the research landscape, establishing clear links between authors, their publications, and research fields.

E.3 Plotting the Author-Article Similarities

In our research, we have developed a method for visualizing the semantic proximity between a specific publication and the top 25 cited author publications across all authors. This is accomplished through a function that maps the abstracts of the documents into a two-dimensional space using Word2Vec for word embeddings and PCA for dimensionality reduction. The resulting plot provides a graphical representation of how closely related the content of a given publication is to the influential works of various authors. In Figure 8 we show an example plot produced using this method.

We invite the reader to observe the distribution of points, where the spatial proximity reflects the semantic similarity between the given publication and the authors' works. This method offers an intuitive way to understand the knowledge structure and the implicit connections between different research articles. We intend to incorporate all the above-mentioned changes into Label Studio to decrease the workload of the annotators and to increase the overall efficiency and accuracy of the process. The authors will be selected through the process of ranking and choosing the one with the highest similarity score for annotating the document. The author will be given a union set of 5 categories with respect to the author's publications and the publication itself to choose from, which align the most with the publication.

F LLM Annotation

F.1 LLM Selection

In our work, we use the weights of the v1.1 model (`https://github.com/lm-sys/FastChat/blob/main/docs/vicuna_weights_version.md`) for Vicuna-7B and 13B. All inference tasks are executed on two sets of RTX 3090 (24GB of memory each). The parameters employed during response generation are as follows: `max_length` set to 100,000, `do_sample` enabled as True, and `temperature` adjusted to 0.7.

Our vision is to build a completely open source pipeline, so we have disregarded LLMs such as GPT-4 (OpenAI, 2023) which only provide API access, instead we have preferred open source alternatives such as LLaMA. We have explored non-LLaMA based LLMs such as OpenChatKit (TogetherComputer, 2023), but we encounter issues related to the stability of their output. We notice that these models sometimes produce inconsistent responses for the same data point (i.e., annotating one publication with keywords and labels), alternating between "Agree" and "Disagree" without providing logically coherent reasoning.

Among the multitude of LLaMA-based LLMs, we identify Vicuna as a model specifically fine-tuned for Question-Answering tasks, making it an apt choice for our project. Furthermore, Vicuna's exceptional performance, underscored by its highest Elo rating in the Chatbot Arena (Zheng et al., 2023), convinces us to choose it as our annotator.

F.2 Single-Label

Figure 9 presents the standardized prompt template we employ to query the LLM regarding its agreement with the category predicted by our model for each data point in the ECON *single-label* dataset. It should be noted that certain segments of the prompts remain fixed and repetitive, a feature we refer to as "instructions". This design is necessitated by the LLM's inherent propensity to forget previous text, meaning that inputting the instruction just once may compromise the quality of responses for subsequent data points. For instance, they might cease to incorporate crucial keywords such as "Agree", "Disagree", "NOT ECON". Therefore, we find it essential to provide an instruction for each data point.

F.3 Multi-Label

For the ECON *multi-label* dataset, we engage the LLM with up to five prompts for each data point (Figure 10). The first prompt asks whether the given abstract is relevant to the field of Economics. If the answer is negative, we terminate further inquiry. However, if the LLM confirms the economic relevance, we proceed to query the model's agreement with up to three categories our model had previously predicted. Lastly, we ask the LLM about any additional categories to which it believes the abstract may belong, beyond those predicted by our model. This final query is intended primarily as a preparatory measure for future keyword analysis. Similarly, the persistent recurrence of identical instructions within the prompt template is designed to mitigate the issue of forgetfulness inherent in the LLM. When we compare the output of the LLM with those of the human annotators on 100 annotations, we see a significant overlap in the categories allotted using both methodologies, which shows the potential to employ LLMs for multi-label tasks.

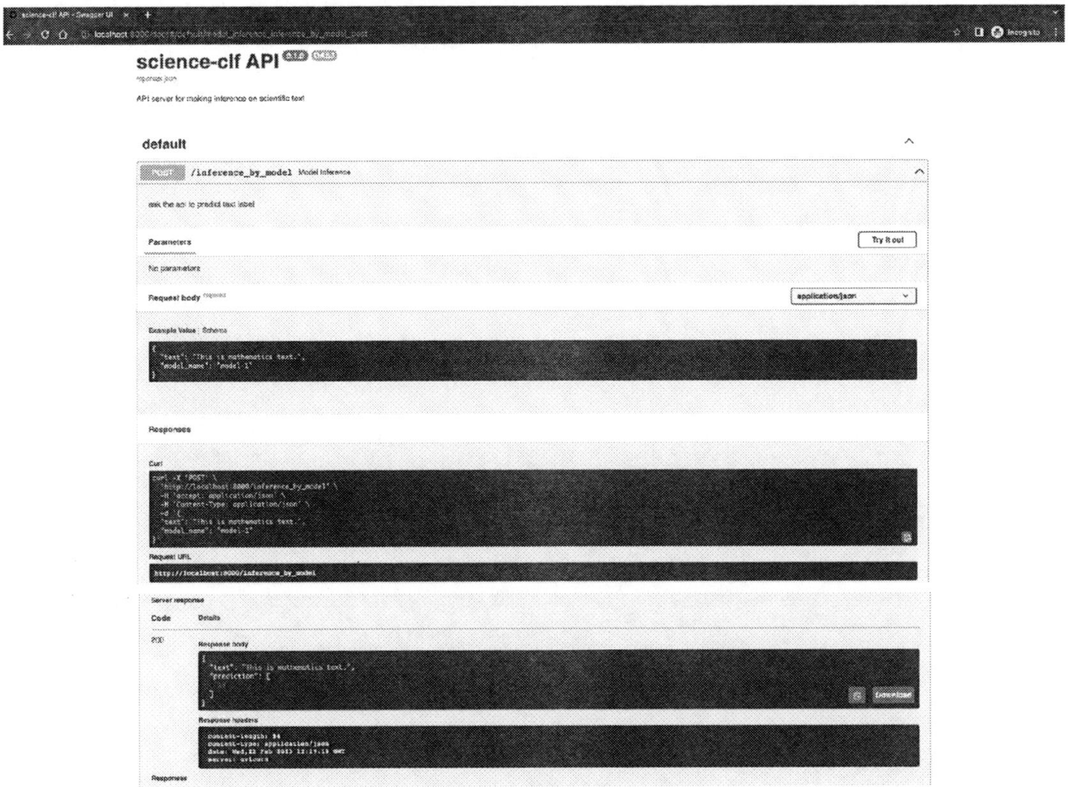

(1) API: `inference_by_model`.

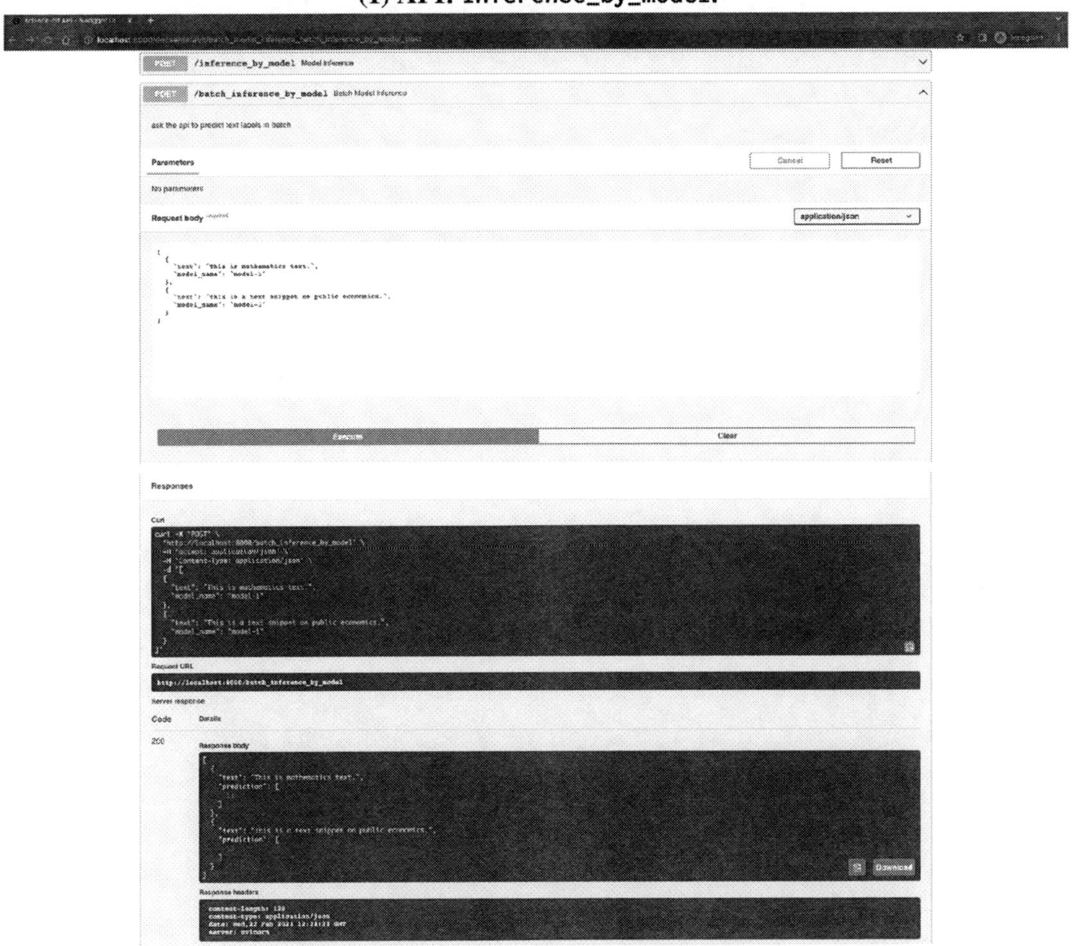

(2) API: `batch_inference_by_model`.

Figure 7: Inference API Calls.

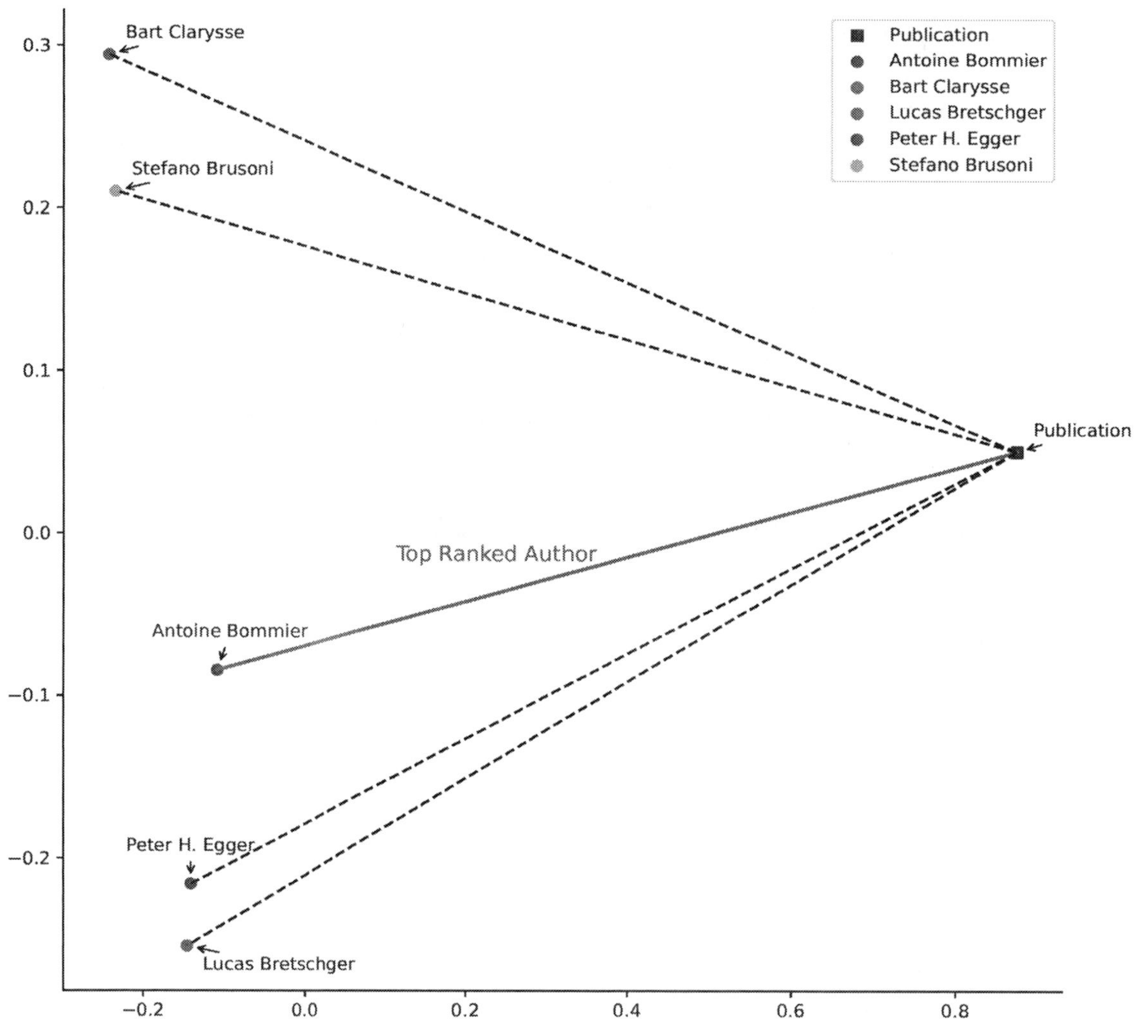

Figure 8: A Two-Dimensional Representation of the Semantic Proximity (between a specific publication and the top 25 cited author publications). Each point represents an author's work, and the spatial distribution reflects the semantic similarity to the given publication.

Prompt: I have trained a machine learning llm whose input is the abstract of a scientific article, and the predicted output is its predicted category.
Candidate categories include: {CAT1_NAMES}.
The abstract is: {abstract}.
My llm-predicted category is: {cat1}.
You have three options: 'Agree, Disagree, NOT ECON'.
Please choose ONLY ONE to output.
If you think this article belongs to the field of economics and the category predicted by the llm is correct, please output 'Agree' and give reasons;
Otherwise, If you think this article belongs to the field of economics but the category predicted by the llm is incorrect, please output 'Disagree', state which category it should belong to according to your opinion, and then provide reasons;
Otherwise, If you think this article does not belong to the field of economics, output 'NOT ECON', and give reasons.

Response: Disagree, Business Administration and Business Economics; Marketing; Accounting; Personnel Economics.
While the article does discuss adsorption/desorption behavior in alluvial soils, it also involves other economic factors such as cation exchange capacity and clay content, as well as the amount of Se desorbed in different forms. These factors suggest that the article may be more relevant to the field of Business Administration and Business Economics, which encompasses topics such as marketing, accounting, and personnel economics. Additionally, the article does not seem to fit squarely into the category of Agricultural and Natural Resource Economics & Environmental and Ecological Economics, as it is not solely focused on environmental or natural resource issues.

Figure 9: LLM Annotation Template for Single-Label Data. {CAT1_NAMES} should be replaced with a string list [Agricultural and Natural Resource Economics; Environmental and Ecological Economics, Industrial Organization, ...], which contains 18 elements (i.e., candidate categories). Taking Paper ID 2279482037 from the ECON single label dataset as an example, replace {abstract} with *Laboratory studies were conducted to investigate the adsorption/desorption behaviour* ... and replace {cat1} with *Agricultural and Natural Resource Economics; Environmental and Ecological Economics*. The response is the Vicuna-13B output for this data point.

1st Prompt: I have trained a machine learning llm whose input is the abstract of a scientific article, and the predicted output is its predicted categories (up to 3).
Candidate categories include: `{CAT1_NAMES}`.
The abstract is: `{abstract}`".
Do you think this abstract belongs to the field of Economics?
If so, output 'Yes'; if not, output 'No'.
1st Response: Yes.

2nd Prompt: The abstract is: `{abstract}`
Do you think this abstract belongs to the first model-predicted category `{cat1}`? If you agree with the first model-predicted category, please output 'Agree' and the reason; if you do not agree with the first model-predicted category, please output 'Disagree' and the reason.
2nd Response: Agree. The abstract describes a theoretical model of a monopoly firm that is introducing a new product with an unknown quality level to consumers. The model predicts that the firm will use price as a signal of quality, and that the price will monotonically increase with the quality level. This model falls within the category of microeconomics, which is concerned with the behavior of firms and consumers in markets, and how government policies can influence that behavior.

3rd Prompt: The abstract is: `{abstract}`
Do you think this abstract belongs to the second model-predicted category `{cat2}`? If you agree with the second model-predicted category, please output 'Agree' and the reason; if you do not agree with the second model-predicted category, please output 'Disagree' and the reason.
3rd Response: Disagree. The abstract does not appear to belong to the category of "History of Economic Thought, Methodology, and Heterodox Approaches." It is more closely related to the category of "Consumer Behavior and Demand Analysis" or "Market Structure and Pricing."

4th Prompt: Are there any other categories that you think are more suitable for this abstract, besides `{cat1}` `{cat2}` `{cat3}`?
If so, please output some other categories among candidate categories `{CAT1_NAMES}` and the reasons. If not, please output the reason why not.
4th Response: Some other categories that might be suitable for this abstract could include:
Agricultural and Natural Resource Economics: This category could be a good fit because the abstract discusses the impact of technology on the agricultural sector, including the use of drones for crop monitoring and automated harvesting.
Environmental and Ecological Economics: This category could also be a good fit because the abstract mentions the potential for drone technology to improve crop yield and reduce the use of pesticides, which could have positive environmental impacts.
However, it is also possible that the abstract could fit into multiple categories, depending on the specific focus of the research. For example, the abstract could be categorized as both Agricultural and Natural Resource Economics and Environmental and Ecological Economics.
Overall, the categories of Business Administration and Business Economics, Mathematical and Quantitative Methods, Public Economics, and International Economics may not be as directly relevant to the focus of the research, although there could still be some overlap depending on the specific focus of the study.

Figure 10: LLM Annotation Template for Multi-Label Data. `{CAT1_NAMES}` should be replaced with the same string list described in Figure 9. Taking Paper ID 1497381249 from the ECON multilabel dataset as an example, replace `{abstract}` with *This paper analyzes the role of price as a signal of the quality of a monopoly firm's new product ...*, `{cat1}` with *Microeconomics*, and `{cat2}` with *History of Economic Thought, Methodology, and Heterodox Approaches*. Since our model only provides two categories, `{cat3}` is an empty string and no prompt is given. All responses are the outputs of Vicuna-13B for this data point.

IFAN: An Explainability-Focused Interaction Framework for Humans and NLP Models

Edoardo Mosca, Daryna Dementieva, Tohid Ebrahim Ajdari,
Maximilian Kummeth, Kirill Gringauz, Yutong Zhou and **Georg Groh**
TU Munich, Department of Informatics, Germany
`{name.surname}@tum.de`
`grohg@in.tum.de`

Abstract

Interpretability and human oversight are fundamental pillars of deploying complex NLP models into real-world applications. However, applying explainability and human-in-the-loop methods requires technical proficiency. Despite existing toolkits for model understanding and analysis, options to integrate human feedback are still limited. We propose IFAN, a framework for real-time explanation-based interaction with NLP models. Through IFAN's interface, users can provide feedback to selected model explanations, which is then integrated through adapter layers to align the model with human rationale. We show the system to be effective in debiasing a hate speech classifier with minimal impact on performance. IFAN also offers a visual admin system and API to manage models (and datasets) as well as control access rights. A demo is live at ifan.ml.

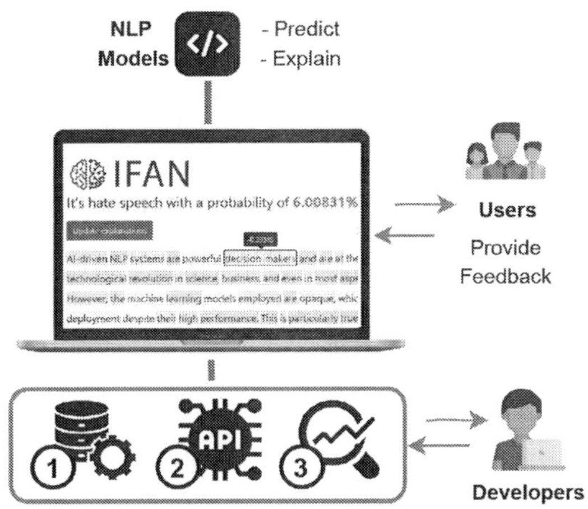

Figure 1: IFAN in brief. The interface allows NLP models and users to interact through predictions, explanations, and feedback. IFAN also provides developers with (1) a manager for models and datasets, (2) model API access, and (3) reports about the model.

1 Introduction

As *Natural Language Processing* (NLP) systems continue to improve in performance, they are increasingly adopted in real-world applications (Khurana et al., 2022). *Large Language Models* (LLMs)—such as GPT-3 (Brown et al., 2020), BLOOM (Scao et al., 2022a), and T5 (Raffel et al., 2020)—are without a shred of doubt the main protagonists of recent advances in the field. They are able to substantially outperform previous solutions while being directly applicable to any NLP task.

There are however strong concerns given the black-box nature of such architectures (Madsen et al., 2022; Mosca et al., 2022a). In fact, their large scale and high complexity are substantial drawbacks in terms of *transparency*, *accountability*, and *human oversight*. Beyond ethical considerations, even legal guidelines from the European Union are now explicitly defining these interpretability factors as essential for any deployed AI system (European Commission, 2020).

Research efforts in *eXplainable Artificial Intelligence* (XAI) (Arrieta et al., 2020; Mosca et al., 2022b) and *Human-in-the-Loop* (HitL) machine learning (Monarch, 2021) have thus been on the rise—producing solutions that aim at mitigating the current lack of interpretability. Most notably, the recent literature contains a number of toolkits and frameworks to analyze, understand, and improve complex NLP models (Wallace et al., 2019; Liu et al., 2021). Some of them even offer low-code interfaces for stakeholders who do not possess the otherwise required technical proficiency. Nonetheless, current options to collect human rationale and provide it as feedback to the model are still limited.

We propose IFAN, a novel low-to-no-code framework to interact in real time with NLP models via explanations. Our contribution can be summarized as follows:

(1) IFAN offers an interface for users to provide feedback to selected model explana-

Proceedings of the 13th International Joint Conference on Natural Language Processing and the 3rd Conference of the Asia-Pacific Chapter of the Association for Computational Linguistics: System Demonstrations, pages 59–76
November 1–4, 2023.

tions, which is then integrated via parameter-efficient adapter layers.

(2) Our live platform also offers a visual administration system and API to manage models, datasets, and users as well as their corresponding access rights.

(3) We show the efficiency of our framework in debiasing a hate speech classifier and propose a feedback-rebalancing step to mitigate the model's forgetfulness across updates.

IFAN's demo is accessible at ifan.ml[1] together with its documentation.[2] Full access is available with login credentials, which we can provide upon request. A supplementary video showcase can be found online[3].

2 Related Work

2.1 HitL with Model Explanations

Human-in-the-Loop (HitL) machine learning studies how models can be continuously improved with human feedback (Monarch, 2021). While a large part of the HitL literature deals with label-focused feedback such as *active learning*, more recent works explore how explanations can be leveraged to provide more detailed human rationale (Lertvittayakumjorn and Toni, 2021).

Combining classical HitL (Wang et al., 2021) with explanations to construct human feedback for the model (Han et al., 2020) has been referred to as *Explanation-Based Human Debugging* (EBHD) (Lertvittayakumjorn and Toni, 2021). Good examples are Ray et al. (2019), Selvaraju et al. (2019), and Strout et al. (2019), which show improvements in performance and interpretability when iteratively providing models with human rationale.

A more NLP-focused EBHD approach is Yao et al. (2021), where the authors leverage explanations to debug and refine two transformer instances—BERT (Devlin et al., 2019) and RoBERTa (Liu et al., 2019). Concretely, word saliency explanations at different levels of granularity are provided to humans, who in turn provide suggestions in the form of natural language. The annotator's feedback is converted into first-order logic rules, which are later utilized to condition learning with new samples.

[1]https://ifan.ml

[2]https://ifan.ml/documentation

[3]https://youtu.be/EzC6HI3JwaQ

2.2 Interactive NLP Analysis Platforms

In the recent literature, we can find strong contributions in terms of software and digital toolkits to analyze and explain NLP models (Wallace et al., 2019; Hoover et al., 2020) as well as further refining them via parameter-efficient fine-tuning (Beck et al., 2022).

For instance, Liu et al. (2021) proposes EXPLAINABOARD, an interactive explainability-focused leaderboard for NLP models. More in detail, it allows researchers to run diagnostics about the strengths and weaknesses of a given model, compare different architectures, and closely analyze predictions as well as recurring model mistakes. Similarly, the LANGUAGE INTERPRETABILITY TOOL by Tenney et al. (2020) is an open-source platform and API to visualize and understand NLP models. In particular, it provides a browser-based interface integrating local explanations as well as counterfactual examples to enable model interpretability and error analysis.

Finally, Beck et al. (2022) releases ADAPTERHUB PLAYGROUND, a no-code platform to few-shot learning with language models. Specifically, the authors built an intuitive interface where users can easily perform predictions and training of complex NLP models on several natural language tasks.

3 IFAN

The **I**nteraction **F**ramework for **A**rtificial and **N**atural Intelligence (**IFAN**) is a web-based platform for inspecting and controlling text processing models. Its main goal is to decrease the opacity of NLP systems and integrate explanation-based HitL into their development pipeline. Through our interface, stakeholders can test and explain models' behavior and—when encountering anomalies in predictions or explanations—they can fix them onsite by providing feedback.

The main blocks of the platform are presented in Figure 2. The **Backbone** part contains all machine learning development components—datasets and models. We adopt HuggingFace formats (see 3.3 and 3.4) (Wolf et al., 2020) and wrap the entire backbone as a Docker[4] image for deployment. The **User Interface** is the visual component of the platform, where all the human-machine interaction takes place. Here, developers have also access to additional visual resources to configure details about models, datasets, and users.

[4]https://www.docker.com

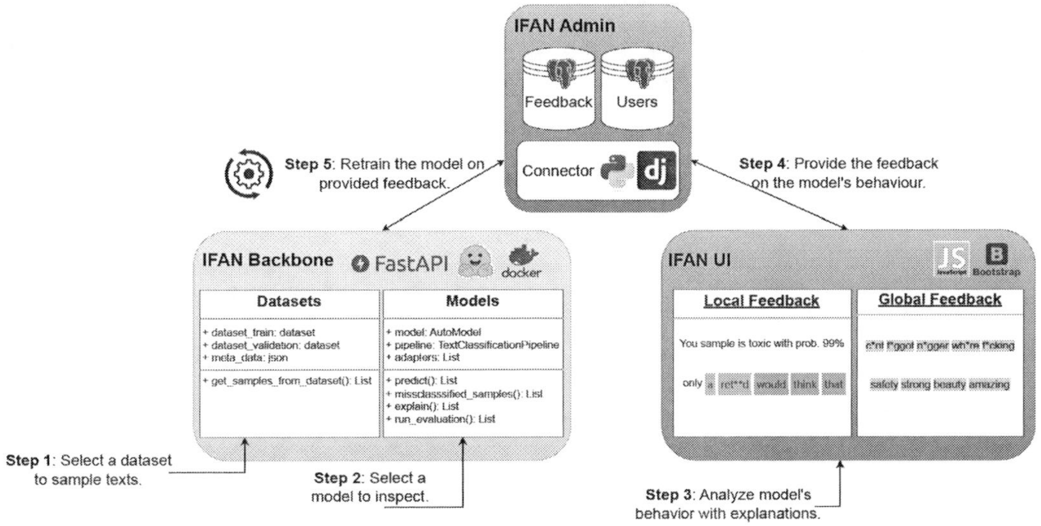

Figure 2: Overall schema of IFAN idea: (i) The user selects a dataset or writes a customized input. (ii) Then the user can select a model which should be inspected. (iii) With the UI, annotators can check the model's prediction on a sample and two types of explanations – local and global. (iv) If there is some misbehavior, the annotators can provide feedback. (v) The feedback is stored and then used to fine-tune the model.

The connection between the backbone and the user interface is managed by the **Admin** component. All the user data and rights as well as samples receiving feedback are stored in a PostgreSQL[5] database instance. The communication is handled via Python Django[6], which integrates everything w.r.t. user authentication, API calls/responses, state logs, and location of backbone resources. In the next sections, we provide a more detailed description of the main platform components.

3.1 User Interface

Our frontend is built with Bootstrap[7] and JavaScript[8]. Currently, the pages available in our UI are the following:

Landing Page Here users can get a short introduction to IFAN. We briefly explain our platform's goals, the concept of HitL, and how our framework can be integrated into the development of NLP models.

Documentation It provides a detailed description of all the UI components together with screenshots and guidelines. Here, users can find specific instructions on how to configure and interact with our platform.

Feedback This is the main interaction page. Here, users can run a model on an input sample either taken from the dataset or that they wrote themselves. Then, they can load the model's prediction and explanations and provide feedback in terms of both the label and features' relevance.

Report This page has limited access (see 3.2). Developers can evaluate models before and after feedback incorporation on a chosen dataset as well as inspect misclassified samples.

Configuration This page has limited access (see 3.2). Here, developers can configure and manage the platform, More specifically, users can be created, modified, and deleted as well as upgraded or downgraded in their roles and access rights. Also, they can manage models and datasets as well as specify the currently active ones.

Account Settings Each authorized user can view, edit, export, and delete their account data (GDPR compliance) as well as reset their login password.

3.2 Users

The platform separates users in three tiers: *developers*, *annotators*, and *unauthorized* users (Table 1).

Unauthorized users do not possess login credentials and have limited access to the platform. They can visualize model predictions and explanations but their feedback is not considered.

[5] https://www.postgresql.org
[6] https://www.djangoproject.com
[7] https://getbootstrap.com
[8] https://www.javascript.com

	Dev	Annotator	Unauthorized
Classification & Explanations	✔	✔	✔
Smart Samples Selection	✔	✔	✘
Feedback	✔	✔	✘
Active Configuration	✔	✘	✘
Model Report & Miscl. Samples	✔	✘	✘
New Models & Datasets Upload	✔	✘	✘
New Users Creation	✔	✘	✘

Table 1: Different levels of access to IFAN.

Normal users (or annotators) are known through their credentials and can thus actively engage with the model. During a HitL iteration, they can use the feedback page with pre-configured datasets and models, test the model on a text sample, view explanations, and provide feedback if needed.

Developers have full access and can configure all aspects of the platform. More specifically, they have access to the *report* and *configuration* pages (see 3.1) and can thus manage anything regarding users, roles, API access, models, and datasets.

3.3 Datasets

Before the model's behavior exploration, the *active dataset* should be specified via the configuration page (see 3.1). This is the dataset from which the text examples for the model testing are sampled.

Dataset	**Short Description**
HateXplain (Mathew et al., 2021)	A dataset for hate speech classification which has 3 classes for hate type detection, the target community classification, and rationales.
GYAFC (Rao and Tetreault, 2018)	Formality detection dataset which corresponds to 2-class classification: formal and informal.

Table 2: Example of datasets tested at IFAN.

We conform to a standard format by using the HuggingFace Datasets library[9]. Developers interacting with our platform are strongly encouraged to adhere to this standard when uploading new datasets and making them available to the interface. Table 2 shows two examples of datasets already available on our platform.

[9]https://huggingface.co/docs/datasets/index

3.4 Models

Analogous to datasets, the *active model* should be specified via the configuration page and should adhere to the HuggingFace Models standard.[10]

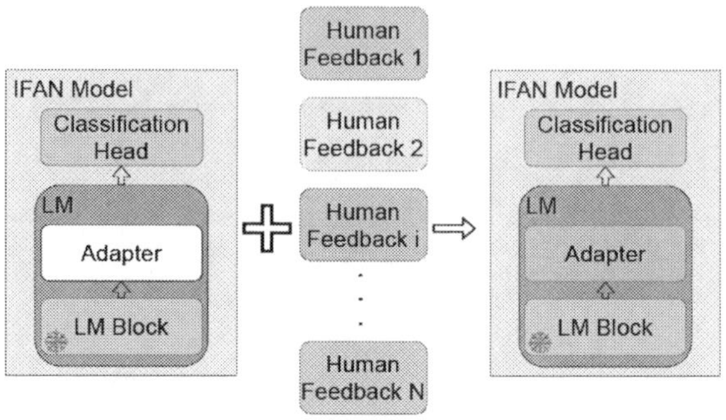

Figure 3: The proposed architecture for the models integrated into IFAN: addition of Adapter layer which is trainable on provided human feedback.

To incorporate feedback into our models, we utilize adapter layers (Houlsby et al., 2019), a parameter-efficient fine-tuning technique. Figure 3 sketches an overview of the architecture used. Adapters are integrated on top of each language model unit (e.g. transformer block) and are trained with the human feedback while we freeze all other model weights. Adapters can also be disabled to recover to the original state of the model.

3.5 Explanations & Feedback Mechanism

Users can evaluate the active model on the active dataset through the Feedback page. They may input text in three ways: i) create a text sample themselves; if authorized: ii) sample a random text from the active dataset; iii) sample a random *misclassified* text from the test part of the active dataset. Users receive the classification results and the model's confidence. They can assess the result and correct any misclassifications.

To further inspect the model's behavior, we provide two types of explanations—local and global. For local explanations on a text sample, we display relevant features to each output class (Figure 4). We attribute scores using the LIME framework (Ribeiro et al., 2016) and—to filter weak correlations—we highlight as relevant only tokens with a score above the threshold $\theta = 0.1$. On the global side, we list the most influential unigrams for each output class. These can be inspected to extract insights about what keywords and patterns

[10]https://huggingface.co/docs/transformers/main_classes/model

the model focuses on at the dataset level. For all 1-grams present in a dataset, their corresponding classification scores are calculated and the tokens with top scores are displayed on the page.

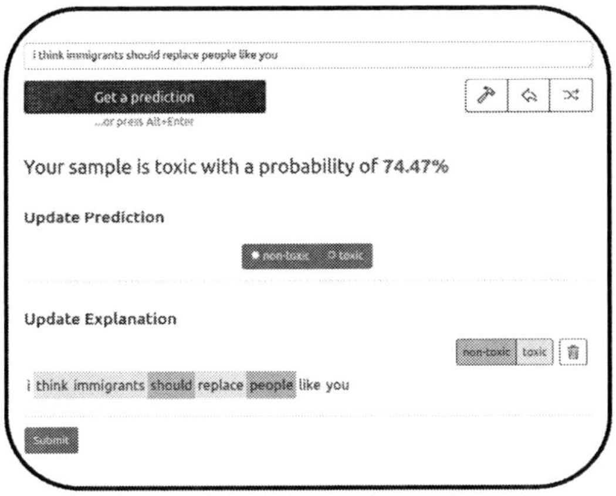

Figure 4: The example of the results and local explanations that annotators can obtain on the Feedback page.

Annotators can easily edit the highlighted tokens and send the updated explanation as feedback. We store the result—i.e. the highlighted relevant parts—and use them to fine-tune the adapter layers. Freezing all other model weights minimizes the computational effort of the feedback step.

Regarding the fine-tuning procedure, directly using the highlighted feedback text for adapter fine-tuning causes significant losses in the original model performance. We propose to mix feedback with original samples to mitigate this effect, which allows effective feedback incorporation while reducing model forgetfulness (see 4 for more details).

3.6 Backbone API

We expose our backbone's API to make available all essential dataset/model management functions. These provide a high-level interface for additional experiments dealing with model evaluation, explanation, and feedback. The API is built with the Python framework FastAPI[11], more details can be found in the Appendix A.

4 Case Study

We carried out a case study to test the applicability of IFAN. We chose a hate speech detection task based on the HateXplain dataset (Mathew et al., 2021). The goal of the experiment was to use our framework to debias a given hate speech detector.

Firstly, we modified the original dataset for binary classification task—*"toxic"* and *"non-toxic"*. We choose the Jewish subgroup as a target for our debiasing process. We fine-tuned BERT (Devlin et al., 2019)[12] and gave feedback to it. Additional experiments with BLOOM and other LLMs are provided in Appendix D and E respectively.

We annotate 24 random misclassified samples, 12 with the most confidence and 12 with the least confidence scores (see Appendix C.1). We invited 3 annotators to participate in the annotation process. The n-grams that were modified by annotators were saved and used to create a new training dataset for the adapters. As a result, we collected 40 annotated n-grams and repeated them to get 120 training samples. To complete the new training creation, we balanced these samples with 500 original samples (250 toxic, 250 non-toxic) randomly selected from the HateXplain dataset.

Model	**Pr**	**Re**	**F1**	**Pr$_J$**
BERT (baseline)	0.80	**0.78**	**0.79**	0.95
Most Confident Missclassified				
BERT+Feedback (non-bal.)	0.34	0.28	0.31	0.82
BERT+Feedback (bal.)	0.78	0.80	**0.79**	**0.97**
Least Confident Missclassified				
BERT+Feedback (non-bal.)	**0.83**	0.73	0.78	0.96
BERT+Feedback (bal.)	0.79	**0.78**	0.78	0.96

Table 3: The results of the case study: hate speech classification model debiasing. We compare different strategies for feedback incorporation. Pr$_J$ states for the Precision score on the Jewish target group.

The results are presented in Table 3. We observe that the non-balanced training dataset, which only contains feedback on the most confidently misclassified samples, resulted in a significant decrease in performance. While the inclusion of feedback on least confident samples caused a slight decline in the overall F1 score, Adapter training on the balanced feedback led to an improvement in the precision score for the Jewish target group.

Figure 5 shows the changes in the detector while fine-tuning with the collected feedback. When rebalancing the feedback, only modified samples are drastically changed while the performance on the original texts is only slightly affected. A detailed comparison between fine-tuning on non-balanced and balanced feedback is in Appendix C.2).

[11]https://fastapi.tiangolo.com

[12]https://huggingface.co/google/bert_uncased_L-2_H-128_A-2

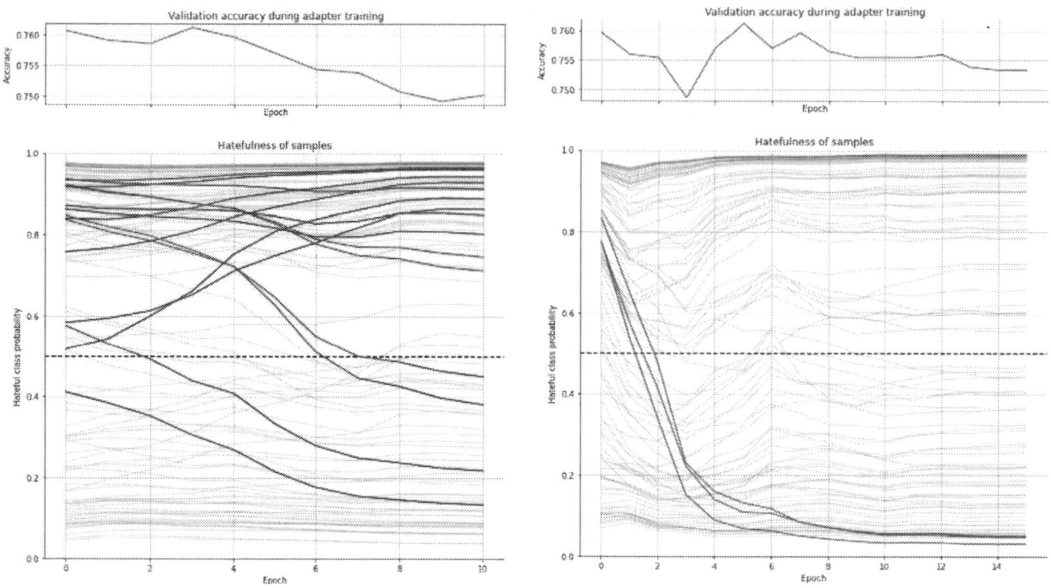

(a) Training on feedback on the Jewish subgroup samples. (b) Training on feedback samples with "jewish" key-words.

Figure 5: Samples confidence variation as the model is fine-tuned with human feedback. The results of the domain case using IFAN platform. We can observe that for both experiments with balanced training data, the overall model's performance is only slightly changed while the model's behavior on the Jewish target group is improved.

5 Limitations & Future Work

As of now, our feedback system is limited to applications in the sequence-to-class format. Work on extending the platform to further task through LLM prompting is currently in progress (see Appendix E).

At the same time, we currently offer a limited set of explanation, feedback, and management options, which we plan to increase in the immediate future. A small user study has been conducted (Appendix B) to collect feedback about the platform and improve its user-friendliness. Our intent is to continue iterating the development of new features with trials with developers and laymen.

Finally, our experiments do not yet show clear trends w.r.t. the correlation between performance and feedback hyperparameters. Indeed, further research and trials have to be carried out to establish optimal choices for the number of feedback samples, fine-tuning epochs, and the rebalancing ratio.

6 Conclusion

This work proposes IFAN, a framework focusing on real-time explanation-based interaction between NLP models and human annotators. Our contribution is motivated by the limited options in terms of existing tools to interpret and control NLP models.

IFAN is composed of three main units. The **Backbone** unifies all the machine learning pipelines and exposes an API for accessibility. The **User Interface**—organized in *landing page*, *documentation*, *feedback*, *report*, and *configuration*—provides an intuitive visual component to interact with models. Finally, the **Admin** controls the connection between the two previous components.

Additionally, we introduce the feedback mechanism that takes advantage of adapter layers to efficiently and iteratively fine-tune models on the downstream task. Our experiments show the frameworks' effectiveness at debiasing a hate speech classifier with minimal performance loss.

We believe IFAN to be a valuable step towards enabling the interpretable and controllable deployment of NLP models—allowing users with no technical proficiency to interact and provide feedback to deployed NLP systems. Regarding future work, we set as a priority to extend the framework to more NLP tasks as well as to integrate additional model analysis features and feedback mechanisms.

Acknowledgments

We thank Natália Souza Soares and Ashish Jha for their valuable contribution. This paper has been supported by the *German Federal Ministry of Education and Research* (BMBF, grant 01IS17049).

Ethical Considerations

In this work, we showed the experiments of hate speech model debasing. The hate speech detection task is the task that requires a lot of attention to provide a fair outcome. One of the issues still is bias, especially against minority groups due to prejudices. We aimed to show an example of how the model can be debiased with respect to some target racial groups. With a conscientious selection of annotators and feedback, we hope that our proposed platform will serve to efficiently adjust NLP models to the diverse world.

For these reasons, we also believe that interpretability and controllability of modern NLP models and systems are fundamental pillars for their ethical and safe deployment (European Commission, 2020). This works aims at having a positive impact on both aspects as it provides a tool to explain models and provide them with feedback. By reducing the technical proficiency required to interact with NLP systems, we hope to facilitate the process of providing valuable human rationales to influence complex models.

Ensuring high quality for the human feedback is challenging (Al Kuwatly et al., 2020), and exposing models to external influence can be used as an exploit by adversarial agents (Mosca et al., 2022a). Especially with a very small crowd of annotators, there's potential for a few people to have a strong influence on the model. A restrictive access rights management system like IFAN's already mitigates these issues. We believe that additional security features as well as tracking annotators' impact are key for future work to foster their trustworthiness.

Previous works mention that users can feel discouraged and frustrated when interacting with poor models and badly-designed interfaces, which can also affect feedback quality (Lertvittayakumjorn and Toni, 2021). This can be addressed by integrating user studies in the development process in order to design more intuitive interfaces and improve the overall user experience.

On the opposite end of the spectrum, plausible explanations can make humans overestimate the model's capabilities and make them trust systems that are still not ready for deployment. In this case, a more diverse and complementary set of explanations for users (Madsen et al., 2022) as well as comprehensive model reports for developers are core goals to provide a more complete picture of the models to be deployed.

References

Hala Al Kuwatly, Maximilian Wich, and Georg Groh. 2020. Identifying and measuring annotator bias based on annotators' demographic characteristics. In *Proceedings of the Fourth Workshop on Online Abuse and Harms*, pages 184–190, Online. Association for Computational Linguistics.

Alejandro Barredo Arrieta, Natalia Díaz-Rodríguez, Javier Del Ser, Adrien Bennetot, Siham Tabik, Alberto Barbado, Salvador García, Sergio Gil-López, Daniel Molina, Richard Benjamins, et al. 2020. Explainable artificial intelligence (xai): Concepts, taxonomies, opportunities and challenges toward responsible ai. *Information Fusion*, 58:82–115.

Tilman Beck, Bela Bohlender, Christina Viehmann, Vincent Hane, Yanik Adamson, Jaber Khuri, Jonas Brossmann, Jonas Pfeiffer, and Iryna Gurevych. 2022. AdapterHub playground: Simple and flexible few-shot learning with adapters. In *Proceedings of the 60th Annual Meeting of the Association for Computational Linguistics: System Demonstrations*, pages 61–75, Dublin, Ireland. Association for Computational Linguistics.

Tom Brown, Benjamin Mann, Nick Ryder, Melanie Subbiah, Jared D Kaplan, Prafulla Dhariwal, Arvind Neelakantan, Pranav Shyam, Girish Sastry, Amanda Askell, et al. 2020. Language models are few-shot learners. *Advances in neural information processing systems*, 33:1877–1901.

Jacob Devlin, Ming-Wei Chang, Kenton Lee, and Kristina Toutanova. 2019. BERT: Pre-training of deep bidirectional transformers for language understanding. In *Proceedings of the 2019 Conference of the North American Chapter of the Association for Computational Linguistics: Human Language Technologies, Volume 1 (Long and Short Papers)*, pages 4171–4186, Minneapolis, Minnesota. Association for Computational Linguistics.

European Commission. 2020. White paper on artificial intelligence: a european approach to excellence and trust. *Com (2020) 65 Final*.

Xiaochuang Han, Byron C. Wallace, and Yulia Tsvetkov. 2020. Explaining black box predictions and unveiling data artifacts through influence functions. In *Proceedings of the 58th Annual Meeting of the Association for Computational Linguistics*, pages 5553–5563, Online. Association for Computational Linguistics.

Benjamin Hoover, Hendrik Strobelt, and Sebastian Gehrmann. 2020. exBERT: A Visual Analysis Tool to Explore Learned Representations in Transformer Models. In *Proceedings of the 58th Annual Meeting of the Association for Computational Linguistics: System Demonstrations*, pages 187–196, Online. Association for Computational Linguistics.

Neil Houlsby, Andrei Giurgiu, Stanislaw Jastrzebski, Bruna Morrone, Quentin de Laroussilhe, Andrea Gesmundo, Mona Attariyan, and Sylvain Gelly. 2019. Parameter-efficient transfer learning for NLP. In *Proceedings of the 36th International Conference on Machine Learning, ICML 2019, 9-15 June 2019, Long Beach, California, USA*, volume 97 of *Proceedings of Machine Learning Research*, pages 2790–2799. PMLR.

Diksha Khurana, Aditya Koli, Kiran Khatter, and Sukhdev Singh. 2022. Natural language processing: State of the art, current trends and challenges. *Multimedia tools and applications*, pages 1–32.

Piyawat Lertvittayakumjorn and Francesca Toni. 2021. Explanation-based human debugging of NLP models: A survey. *Transactions of the Association for Computational Linguistics*, 9:1508–1528.

Pengfei Liu, Jinlan Fu, Yang Xiao, Weizhe Yuan, Shuaichen Chang, Junqi Dai, Yixin Liu, Zihuiwen Ye, and Graham Neubig. 2021. ExplainaBoard: An explainable leaderboard for NLP. In *Proceedings of the 59th Annual Meeting of the Association for Computational Linguistics and the 11th International Joint Conference on Natural Language Processing: System Demonstrations*, pages 280–289, Online. Association for Computational Linguistics.

Yinhan Liu, Myle Ott, Naman Goyal, Jingfei Du, Mandar Joshi, Danqi Chen, Omer Levy, Mike Lewis, Luke Zettlemoyer, and Veselin Stoyanov. 2019. Roberta: A robustly optimized bert pretraining approach. *arXiv preprint arXiv:1907.11692*.

Andreas Madsen, Siva Reddy, and Sarath Chandar. 2022. Post-hoc interpretability for neural nlp: A survey. *ACM Comput. Surv.*, 55(8).

Binny Mathew, Punyajoy Saha, Seid Muhie Yimam, Chris Biemann, Pawan Goyal, and Animesh Mukherjee. 2021. Hatexplain: A benchmark dataset for explainable hate speech detection. In *Thirty-Fifth AAAI Conference on Artificial Intelligence, AAAI 2021, Thirty-Third Conference on Innovative Applications of Artificial Intelligence, IAAI 2021, The Eleventh Symposium on Educational Advances in Artificial Intelligence, EAAI 2021, Virtual Event, February 2-9, 2021*, pages 14867–14875. AAAI Press.

Robert Munro Monarch. 2021. *Human-in-the-Loop Machine Learning: Active learning and annotation for human-centered AI.* Simon and Schuster.

Edoardo Mosca, Shreyash Agarwal, Javier Rando Ramírez, and Georg Groh. 2022a. "that is a suspicious reaction!": Interpreting logits variation to detect NLP adversarial attacks. In *Proceedings of the 60th Annual Meeting of the Association for Computational Linguistics (Volume 1: Long Papers)*, pages 7806–7816, Dublin, Ireland. Association for Computational Linguistics.

Edoardo Mosca, Ferenc Szigeti, Stella Tragianni, Daniel Gallagher, and Georg Groh. 2022b. SHAP-based explanation methods: A review for NLP interpretability. In *Proceedings of the 29th International Conference on Computational Linguistics*, pages 4593–4603, Gyeongju, Republic of Korea. International Committee on Computational Linguistics.

Colin Raffel, Noam Shazeer, Adam Roberts, Katherine Lee, Sharan Narang, Michael Matena, Yanqi Zhou, Wei Li, and Peter J. Liu. 2020. Exploring the limits of transfer learning with a unified text-to-text transformer. *J. Mach. Learn. Res.*, 21:140:1–140:67.

Sudha Rao and Joel Tetreault. 2018. Dear sir or madam, may I introduce the GYAFC dataset: Corpus, benchmarks and metrics for formality style transfer. In *Proceedings of the 2018 Conference of the North American Chapter of the Association for Computational Linguistics: Human Language Technologies, Volume 1 (Long Papers)*, pages 129–140, New Orleans, Louisiana. Association for Computational Linguistics.

Arijit Ray, Yi Yao, Rakesh Kumar, Ajay Divakaran, and Giedrius Burachas. 2019. Can you explain that? lucid explanations help human-ai collaborative image retrieval. In *Proceedings of the AAAI Conference on Human Computation and Crowdsourcing*, volume 7, pages 153–161.

Marco Tulio Ribeiro, Sameer Singh, and Carlos Guestrin. 2016. " why should i trust you?" explaining the predictions of any classifier. In *Proceedings of the 22nd ACM SIGKDD international conference on knowledge discovery and data mining*, pages 1135–1144.

Teven Le Scao, Angela Fan, Christopher Akiki, Ellie Pavlick, Suzana Ilic, Daniel Hesslow, Roman Castagné, Alexandra Sasha Luccioni, François Yvon, Matthias Gallé, Jonathan Tow, Alexander M. Rush, Stella Biderman, Albert Webson, Pawan Sasanka Ammanamanchi, Thomas Wang, Benoît Sagot, Niklas Muennighoff, Albert Villanova del Moral, Olatunji Ruwase, Rachel Bawden, Stas Bekman, Angelina McMillan-Major, Iz Beltagy, Huu Nguyen, Lucile Saulnier, Samson Tan, Pedro Ortiz Suarez, Victor Sanh, Hugo Laurençon, Yacine Jernite, Julien Launay, Margaret Mitchell, Colin Raffel, Aaron Gokaslan, Adi Simhi, Aitor Soroa, Alham Fikri Aji, Amit Alfassy, Anna Rogers, Ariel Kreisberg Nitzav, Canwen Xu, Chenghao Mou, Chris Emezue, Christopher Klamm, Colin Leong, Daniel van Strien, David Ifeoluwa Adelani, and et al. 2022a. BLOOM: A 176b-parameter open-access multilingual language model. *CoRR*, abs/2211.05100.

Teven Le Scao, Angela Fan, Christopher Akiki, Ellie Pavlick, Suzana Ilic, Daniel Hesslow, Roman Castagné, Alexandra Sasha Luccioni, François Yvon, Matthias Gallé, Jonathan Tow, Alexander M. Rush, Stella Biderman, Albert Webson, Pawan Sasanka Ammanamanchi, Thomas Wang, Benoît Sagot, Niklas Muennighoff, Albert Villanova del Moral, Olatunji

Ruwase, Rachel Bawden, Stas Bekman, Angelina McMillan-Major, Iz Beltagy, Huu Nguyen, Lucile Saulnier, Samson Tan, Pedro Ortiz Suarez, Victor Sanh, Hugo Laurençon, Yacine Jernite, Julien Launay, Margaret Mitchell, Colin Raffel, Aaron Gokaslan, Adi Simhi, Aitor Soroa, Alham Fikri Aji, Amit Alfassy, Anna Rogers, Ariel Kreisberg Nitzav, Canwen Xu, Chenghao Mou, Chris Emezue, Christopher Klamm, Colin Leong, Daniel van Strien, David Ifeoluwa Adelani, and et al. 2022b. BLOOM: A 176b-parameter open-access multilingual language model. *CoRR*, abs/2211.05100.

Ramprasaath R Selvaraju, Stefan Lee, Yilin Shen, Hongxia Jin, Shalini Ghosh, Larry Heck, Dhruv Batra, and Devi Parikh. 2019. Taking a hint: Leveraging explanations to make vision and language models more grounded. In *Proceedings of the IEEE International Conference on Computer Vision*, pages 2591–2600.

Julia Strout, Ye Zhang, and Raymond Mooney. 2019. Do human rationales improve machine explanations? In *Proceedings of the 2019 ACL Workshop BlackboxNLP: Analyzing and Interpreting Neural Networks for NLP*, pages 56–62, Florence, Italy. Association for Computational Linguistics.

Ian Tenney, James Wexler, Jasmijn Bastings, Tolga Bolukbasi, Andy Coenen, Sebastian Gehrmann, Ellen Jiang, Mahima Pushkarna, Carey Radebaugh, Emily Reif, and Ann Yuan. 2020. The language interpretability tool: Extensible, interactive visualizations and analysis for NLP models. In *Proceedings of the 2020 Conference on Empirical Methods in Natural Language Processing: System Demonstrations*, pages 107–118, Online. Association for Computational Linguistics.

Eric Wallace, Jens Tuyls, Junlin Wang, Sanjay Subramanian, Matt Gardner, and Sameer Singh. 2019. AllenNLP interpret: A framework for explaining predictions of NLP models. In *Proceedings of the 2019 Conference on Empirical Methods in Natural Language Processing and the 9th International Joint Conference on Natural Language Processing (EMNLP-IJCNLP): System Demonstrations*, pages 7–12, Hong Kong, China. Association for Computational Linguistics.

Zijie J. Wang, Dongjin Choi, Shenyu Xu, and Diyi Yang. 2021. Putting humans in the natural language processing loop: A survey. In *Proceedings of the First Workshop on Bridging Human–Computer Interaction and Natural Language Processing*, pages 47–52, Online. Association for Computational Linguistics.

Thomas Wolf, Lysandre Debut, Victor Sanh, Julien Chaumond, Clement Delangue, Anthony Moi, Pierric Cistac, Tim Rault, Remi Louf, Morgan Funtowicz, Joe Davison, Sam Shleifer, Patrick von Platen, Clara Ma, Yacine Jernite, Julien Plu, Canwen Xu, Teven Le Scao, Sylvain Gugger, Mariama Drame, Quentin Lhoest, and Alexander Rush. 2020. Transformers: State-of-the-art natural language processing. In *Proceedings of the 2020 Conference on Empirical Methods in Natural Language Processing: System Demonstrations*, pages 38–45, Online. Association for Computational Linguistics.

Huihan Yao, Ying Chen, Qinyuan Ye, Xisen Jin, and Xiang Ren. 2021. Refining language models with compositional explanations. *Advances in Neural Information Processing Systems*, 34:8954–8967.

A Backbone API Endpoints

Figure 6 shows the auto-generated docs for our backbone's REST API, which serves as guidelines to interact with our backbone. Endpoints are divided into functional groups—*models*, *datasets*, *prediction*, *explanation*, and *feedback*). Currently, this page is only accessible within our institution's network for security reasons.

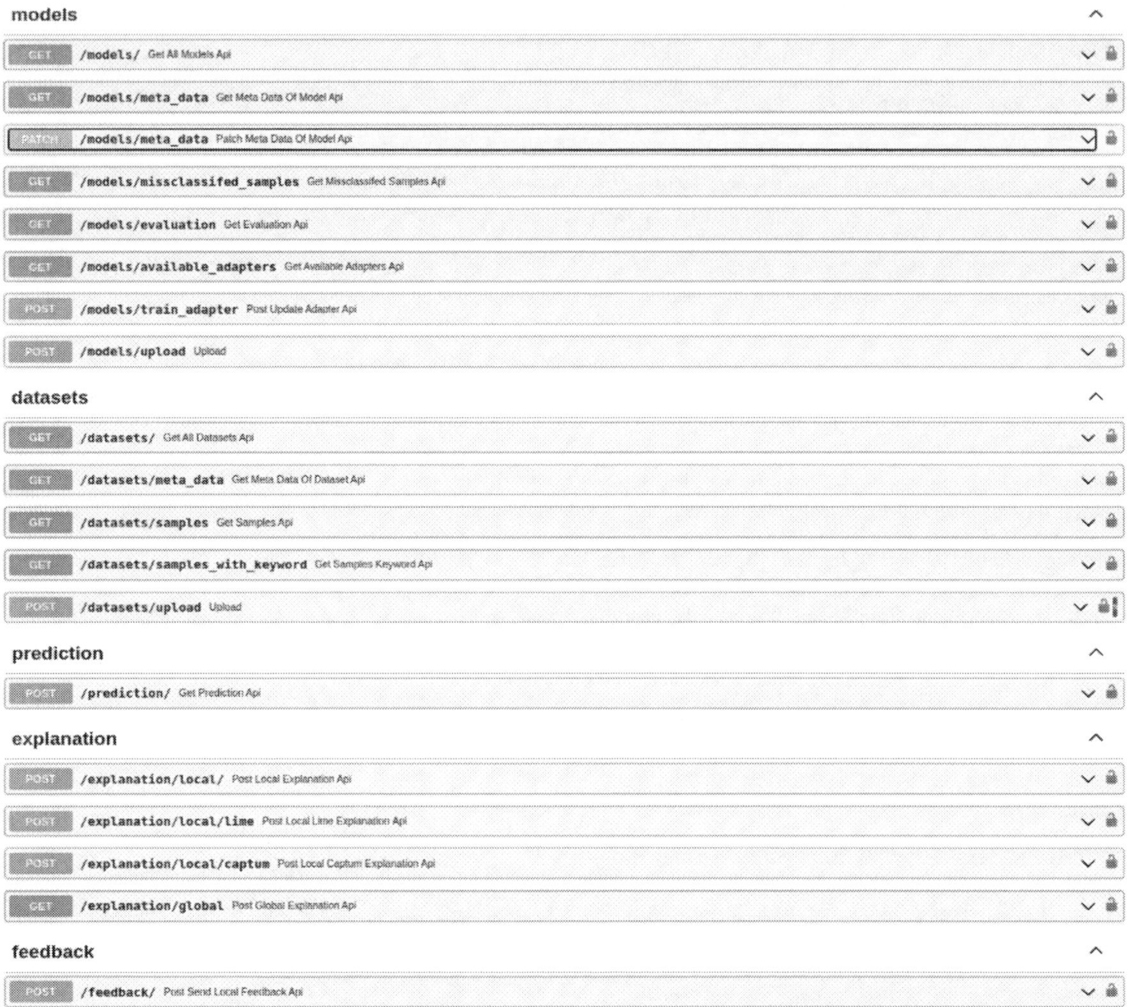

Figure 6: Screenshot of the Swagger UI for our backbone API endpoints.

Developers with direct API access (specifiable on the *configuration page*, see 3.1) can directly make requests to this high-level interface for additional (larger-scale) experiments. Once again, the API has been built with the Python framework FastAPI[13].

Figure 7 shows the documentation for the *explanation* endpoint. Here, we can inspect the details about the endpoint, such as the required parameters—i.e. the path to the model, the explainer to be used (e.g. LIME), and the model's prediction as body request.

[13]https://fastapi.tiangolo.com

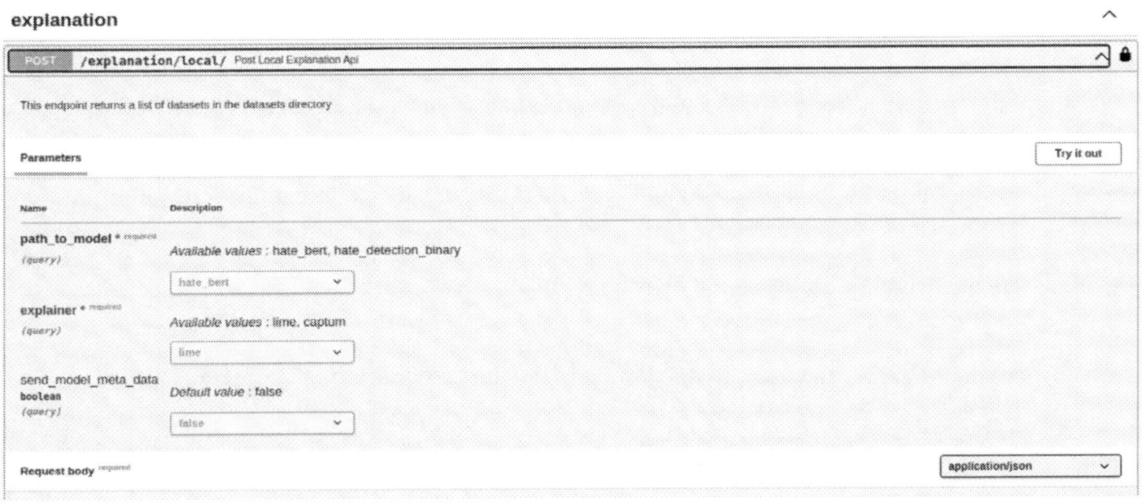

Figure 7: Screenshot of the *explanation* endpoint from our backbone API's Swagger UI.

B User Study

We performed a small user study evaluating the usability of our platform with users having different backgrounds. We gathered a total of nine testers, which we organize into three different categories based on their familiarity with the underlying methodologies. Users may be *laymen*, *computer scientists*, or *experts*. For each of these categories, three testers are assigned. Laymen are general users with no exposure to computer science. Computer scientists are those who studied computer science or a related discipline and who work in corresponding fields, such as software development. People who also possess knowledge in the domains of machine learning and NLP are considered experts.

We asked the users to try out to interact with IFAN and then answer several questions about the website's usability. The questionnaire was of the following structure:

- The first question is about the competency of the test person, which is categorized as computer science, natural language processing expert, or layman.

- Users assign a score between 1 and 5 to the local explanation on the left side of the feedback page.

- A textual input field for the users to hand in more detailed feedback on the previous rating.

- Users assign a score between 1 and 5 to the global explanation on the right side of the feedback page.

- A textual input field for the users to hand in more detailed feedback on the previous rating.

- Users rate the overall usability of the website with a score between 1 and 5.

- A textual input field for the users to hand in more detailed feedback on the previous rating.

The average ratings given by users: (i) Local explanation: 3.88; (ii) Global explanation: 3.2; (iii) General usability: 3.33. The problem that the users mentioned were insufficiency of only one form of explanations and feedback, sometimes misleading interface for markup, and waiting time. While some of the problems are already fixed in the current version of the platform, we are planning to consistently improve the usability of the platform. At the same time, we note a positive result—the users with different backgrounds were overall comfortable with IFAN usage and found it useful to increase the controllability of NLP models. We believe this confirms the possibility of IFAN utilization for stakeholders, developers, and annotators in future applications.

C Case Study

In this section, we provide additional information about the experiment conducted under Case Study (Section 4).

C.1 Annotated Samples *(Warning: the section contains hate speech only with illustrative purposes. We have no intention to offend the reader and a target racial group.)*

Here, we provide the list of that were used for manual annotation (Section 4). These samples were misclassified by hate speech detection model. In Table 4, we provide the misclassified samples with the lowest confidence, in Table 5 – with the highest confidence. All the samples and their true labels are taken from the original HateXplain dataset (Mathew et al., 2021). For the label assignment details, refer to the HateXplain dataset description.

Sample	Original Label	Prediction	Confidence Score
it not so much about the torah which is pretty innocuous and ignored by many jews despite what is said it really about that forbidden book the talmud or babylonian talmud which as goyim cattle we are not permitted to even read good luck with your research	non-toxic	toxic	0.56
if memory serves ashkenazi jews and east asians have higher average iqs	non-toxic	toxic	0.57
speaking of does anyone know which goy group the jews intermarry with in the greatest numbers i was under the impression it was either asians or catholics	toxic	non-toxic	0.52
<user> the jews faked the moon landing	toxic	non-toxic	0.52
<user> <user> she will blame it on jews or trump i bet	toxic	non-toxic	0.53
christianity role is historical protector of the jews it has afforded the tribe the time and space it needed to prepare white genocide teamwhite	toxic	non-toxic	0.54
the jews are gearing up to help usher in democrats in <number> twitter facebook msm google youtube all upping their censorships of the right pro whites	toxic	non-toxic	0.51
amusing to think that white people will never be given a referendum on expelling the jews from our nations when you think about things in such terms it becomes abundantly clear that we are expected by our governments to suffer jewish parasitism without the right to defend ourselves	toxic	non-toxic	0.50
it all hehe haha until we show up at your local favorite hang out spot and wait for you to come out in the van they go one little heeb at a time whatever it takes	toxic	non-toxic	0.53
<user> <user> jews and the stupid holocaust myth	toxic	non-toxic	0.52
<user> jews will never be on the blockchain because you can not trust them	toxic	non-toxic	0.51
<user> <user> it the jews not europeans stop shifting blame on gentiles	toxic	non-toxic	0.57

Table 4: Misclassified with the lowest confidence samples used for manual annotation.

Sample	Original Label	Prediction	Confidence Score
would rather have terrorism over not being able to boycott an allied country this talking point must be important because he repeats it but i can not make out what on earth it supposed to mean if you do not buy stuff from jews they will fake arabs taking down more nyc landmarks	non-toxic	toxic	0.72
how long will jews be a majority in israel	non-toxic	toxic	0.88
what do you mean goes and buys their house not only predates the ghetto it was there before ghetto people came to exist why do you want white people to take a stand for their home but jews to flee theirs	non-toxic	toxic	0.77
calling me a kike is not an insult	non-toxic	toxic	0.97
the jews and muslims grew up together and the jews gave birth to christianity catholicism and later on mormonism like a big religion family	non-toxic	toxic	0.78
greg susan frank rodrick and manny heffley are all jews	non-toxic	toxic	0.67
it amazing how long <user> talked without giving any answers i learned way more about <user> thoughts and life than sargon i thought only jews could bloviate that hard hm	toxic	non-toxic	0.95
<user> <user> um akshually star trek were the space commies and star wars jedis are just space jews	toxic	non-toxic	0.87
<user> apparently not so obvious to some esp the homosexual jewish media that wants women to look like boys and people who think that is traditional rather than feminist	toxic	non-toxic	0.84
sorry i was referring to the holocaust story i believe it to be a lie	toxic	non-toxic	0.89
i swear college is a hot house full of judaised professors with white youth being indoctrinated into this nonsense or have live there days out in fear of being ousted as racists and proud members of white race	toxic	non-toxic	0.90
a few months ago i said that anti semitism doesnt exists naming a group of people is a branch of social sciences called sociology well jews are at war with social sciences now you simply cant name them	toxic	non-toxic	0.74

Table 5: Misclassified with the highest confidence samples used for manual annotation.

C.2 Feedback Mechanisms Comparison

In Section 4, we report the results of the model trained on feedback in two setups: (i) without balancing and (ii) with balancing via using original samples from HateXplain dataset. The comparison between these two setups is visualized in Figures 8 and 9. We tested our approach on the local feedback on the Jewish target group samples as well as samples containing the "Jewish" keyword. For both setups, with balancing, the training procedure runs more stable. The model's performance on other samples from HateXplain dataset changes slightly and the adjustment of its behavior on the marked-up samples proceeds more rapidly.

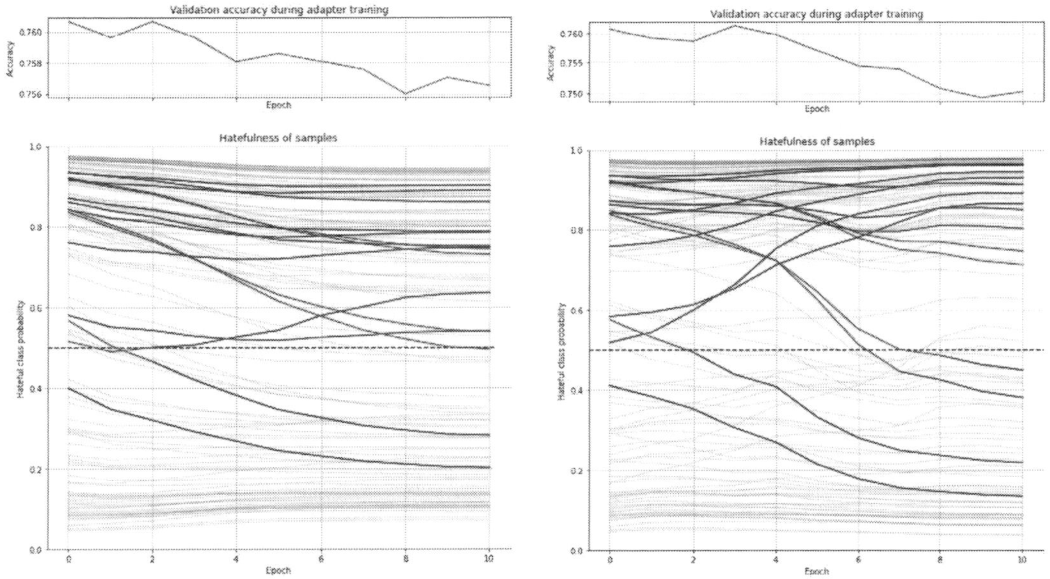

(a) Training without feedback balancing.

(b) Training with feedback balancing.

Figure 8: The comparison of training procedure with and without feedback balancing. Here, the results of local feedback on the least confident misclassified samples from the Jewish target group are shown. We can observe that training with a balanced dataset runs more stable without significant influence on the overall model's domain knowledge.

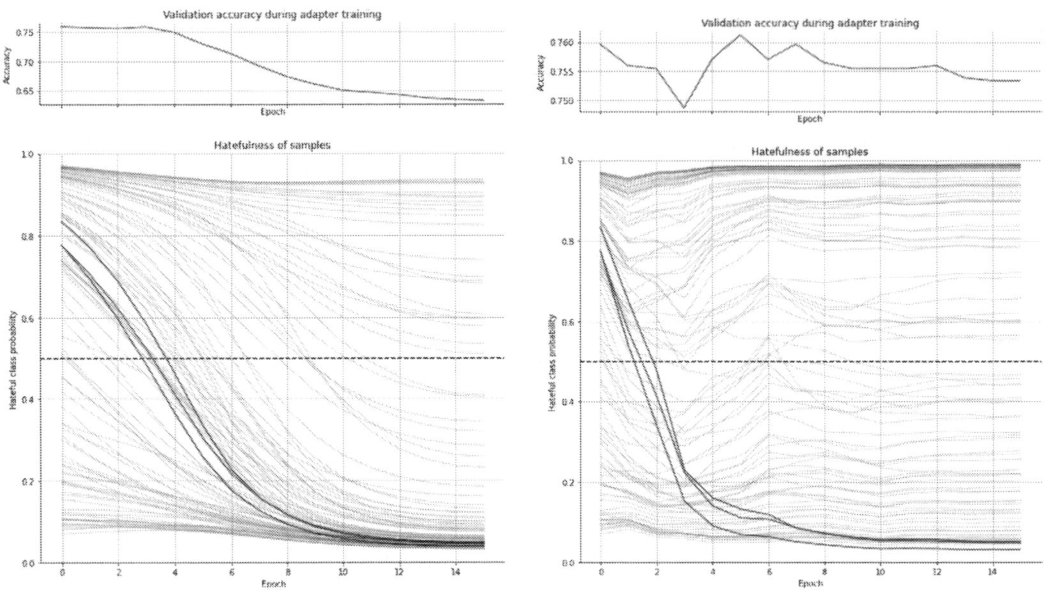

(a) Training without feedback balancing.

(b) Training with feedback balancing.

Figure 9: The comparison of training procedure with and without feedback balancing. Here, the results of local feedback on misclassified samples with "jewish" keywords are shown. We can observe that training with rebalanced dataset runs more stable without significant influence on the overall model's domain knowledge.

D BLOOM for Hate Speech Classification and Human Feedback Incorporation

In addition to the results with BERT for hate speech classification (Section 4), we provide the results of experiments with a BLOOM[14] model (Scao et al., 2022b) (Table 6). Once again, the fine-tuning of adapter layer with human feedback improves model performance within Jewish target group. In the case of BLOOM, the overall F1 score is also improved, confirming the utility of human feedback usage and the possibility of it being extended to other models. Also, from Figure 10, we can see how the label of the misclassified samples (i.e. *"Um ... he's jewish, not Muslim"*) is changing as the model is fine-tuned with the provided feedback.

Model	Pr	Rc	F1	$F1_J$
BLOOM (baseline)	0.40	**0.70**	0.48	0.48
BLOOM+Feedback	**0.49**	0.58	**0.51**	**0.53**

Table 6: The results of the LLMs inference for hate speech classification. $F1_J$ states for the F1 score on the Jewish target group.

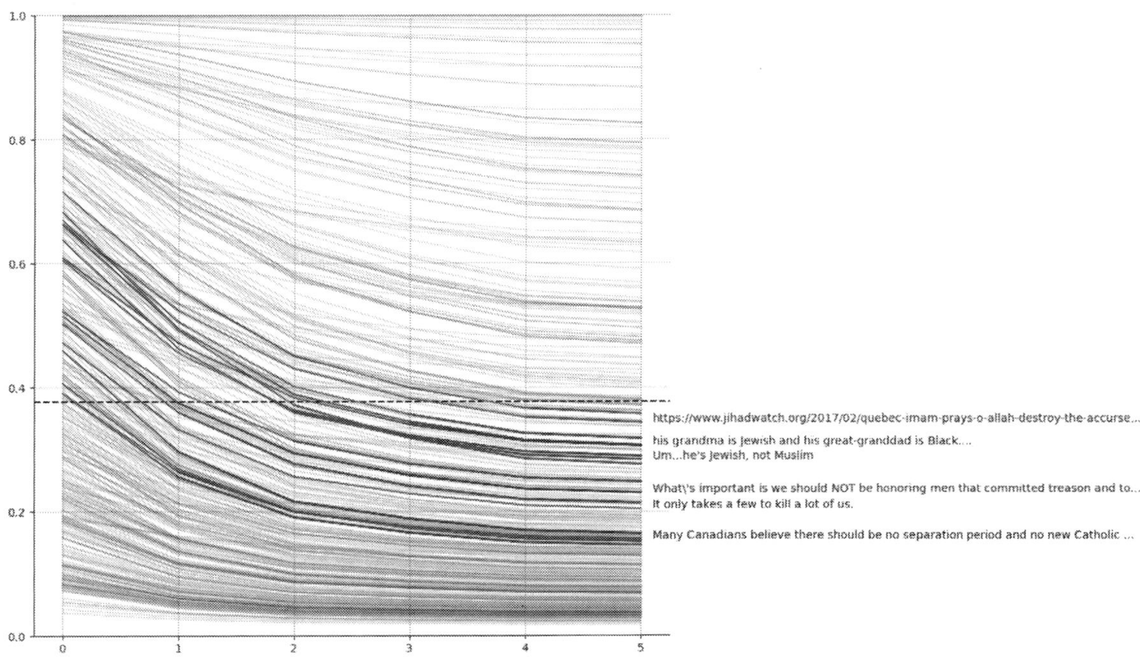

Figure 10: The tracking procedure of the misclassified samples label fix during feedback incorporation.

E Large Language Models for Hate Speech Classification and Explanation

In addition to the classification via linear layers on top of transformer blocks, we test the possibility of large language models to perform text classification and explain their prediction. Potentially, this approach allows further work to extend the framework to any arbitrary NLP tasks.

Currently, the models available on IFAN for testing are: vicgalle/gpt2-alpaca[15], chavinlo/alpaca-native[16], and chavinlo/gpt4-x-alpaca.[17] Their results on hate speech classification task based on HateXapline dataset (Mathew et al., 2021) are presented in Table 7.

For each model, we optimize the prompts to perform hate speech detection:

[14]https://huggingface.co/bigscience/bloom-560m
[15]https://huggingface.co/vicgalle/gpt2-alpaca
[16]https://huggingface.co/chavinlo/alpaca-native
[17]https://huggingface.co/chavinlo/gpt4-x-alpaca

vicgalle/gpt2-alpaca *Instruction: perform the text-classification task on the text using the following labels: 0 or 1. Text: would be hilarious if the un building was turned into homeless shelter or hell why not a refugee center The text is 0 Text: [DATASET SAMLPE] The text is 1 Text: [INPUT TEXT] The text is*

chavinlo/alpaca-native *This is an overall text-classification. For the given TEXT, CLASSIFY the LABEL of that.The LABEL can be 0 or 1. Just output the LABEL. NOTHING ELSE! TEXT: [5 DATASET SAMLPES] LABEL: 0 TEXT: [5 DATASET SAMLPES] LABEL: 1 TEXT: [INPUT TEXT]. LABEL:*

chavinlo/gpt4-x-alpaca *INSTRUCTION: Given the following DATASET DESCRIPTION, EXTRACT the TASK of it, and PERFORM the TASK on the INPUT TEXT. The FINAL LABEL could be 0 or 1. Just output the FINAL LABEL. NOTHING ELSE! DATASET DESCRIPTION: Hatexplain is the first benchmark hate speech dataset covering multiple aspects of the issue. Each post in the dataset is annotated from three different perspectives: the basic, commonly used 3-class classification (i.e., hate, offensive or normal), the target community (i.e., the community that has been the victim of hate speech/offensive speech in the post), and the rationales, i.e., the portions of the post on which their labelling decision (as hate, offensive or normal) is based. CONTEXT: TEXT: [DATASET SAMPLE] FINAL LABEL: 0 TEXT: [DATASET SAMPLE] FINAL LABEL: 1 INPUT TEXT: TEXT: [INPUT TEXT]. FINAL LABEL:*

Despite the specific differences in the various prompts, they all follow the core idea of i) mention the main task which can be extracted from the dataset metadata; ii) provide the general information about labels; iii) provide some examples for each label from the dataset. Potentially, this prompt design can be used for any classification task.

Model	Pr	Re	F1
vicgalle/gpt2-alpaca	0.63	0.56	0.59
chavinlo/alpaca-native	0.60	0.51	0.55
chavinlo/gpt4-x-alpaca	**0.66**	**0.63**	**0.64**

Table 7: The results of the LLMs inference for hate speech classification.

F Supplementary Video Demo

A supplementary video showcase can be found on Youtube[18]. For completeness, we also point at an additional version of such demo, as well on Youtube[19], dating back to March 2023.

[18] https://youtu.be/EzC6HI3JwaQ

[19] https://www.youtube.com/watch?v=BzzoQzTsrLo

WAMP: Writing, Annotation, and Marking Platform

Geonsik Moon*, **Muhammad Reza Qorib***, **Daniel Dahlmeier**† and **Hwee Tou Ng***
* Department of Computer Science, National University of Singapore
† SAP Innovation Center Singapore
moon97@nus.edu.sg, mrqorib@comp.nus.edu.sg, nght@comp.nus.edu.sg
d.dahlmeier@sap.com

Abstract

Creating annotated corpora has always been one of the major challenges for grammatical error correction (GEC). Annotated corpora are critical since they enable us to evaluate the accuracy of GEC systems by providing gold-standard references. In this paper, we propose a web-based annotation tool – Writing, Annotation, and Marking Platform (WAMP) – that tackles this issue of generating annotated corpora by allowing annotators to annotate essays with ease and export the resulting annotated essays for use in GEC research. The source code and a demo video of WAMP are publicly available at: https://github.com/nusnlp/wamp.

1 Introduction

Grammar is an important part of language learning, especially in writing. Incorrect grammar could misrepresent some of the meanings that a writer is trying to convey and damage the credibility of the writer, ultimately resulting in ineffective communication. Despite having learned English in primary and secondary education, non-native English speakers can still struggle with grammatical errors in writing. Subject-verb agreement and verb tense are among the most frequent error types (Singh et al., 2017). As such, grammatical error correction (GEC), formulated as the task of automatically detecting and correcting grammatical errors in a text (Chollampatt et al., 2016; Chollampatt and Ng, 2018; Qorib et al., 2022; Bryant et al., 2023), has gained attention over the past decade as a useful application for language learners. GEC facilitates faster language learning by providing a better alternative for these students to check their writing, replacing manual checking.

However, one of the biggest challenges for GEC arises from generating high-quality annotated corpora. Due to its time-consuming nature, manual annotation is still regarded as the major bottleneck for building annotated corpora that are large enough to train and test systems for many NLP tasks (Neves and Ševa, 2019). GEC is no exception, as it also requires a gold-standard reference in order to evaluate the accuracy of GEC systems and analyze the specific areas in which these systems under-perform. The NUS Corpus of Learner English (NUCLE) (Dahlmeier et al., 2013), a large annotated corpus of learner essays, was created in collaboration with the Centre for English Language Communication (CELC) at NUS. Comprising about 1,400 essays written by undergraduate students at NUS, NUCLE contains a total of over one million words which were annotated with error tags and corrections by a team of professional English language instructors at NUS (Dahlmeier et al., 2013). In building the NUCLE corpus, a web-based annotation tool – Writing, Annotation, and Marking Platform (WAMP) – was utilized to allow the instructors to annotate student essays online, using a web browser of their choice.

To facilitate the creation of additional annotated corpora for GEC, we provide the system overview, functionalities, and system implementation of WAMP in this paper. We also introduce two new enhancements to the original WAMP that allow greater usability of the tool for GEC research: (1) The user can choose from different sets of error tags that are available for annotators. (2) The user can export each annotated essay into the M2 file format, which displays the start word index, end word index, and the error type of each edit. This M2 file can then be used as a gold-standard reference for the MaxMatch (M^2) scorer (Dahlmeier and Ng, 2012) and the ERRANT (Bryant et al., 2017) scorer to evaluate GEC systems.

2 System Overview

Writing, Annotation, and Marking Platform (WAMP) is a web-based annotation tool, built us-

Proceedings of the 13th International Joint Conference on Natural Language Processing and the 3rd Conference of the Asia-Pacific Chapter of the Association for Computational Linguistics: System Demonstrations, pages 77–85
November 1–4, 2023.

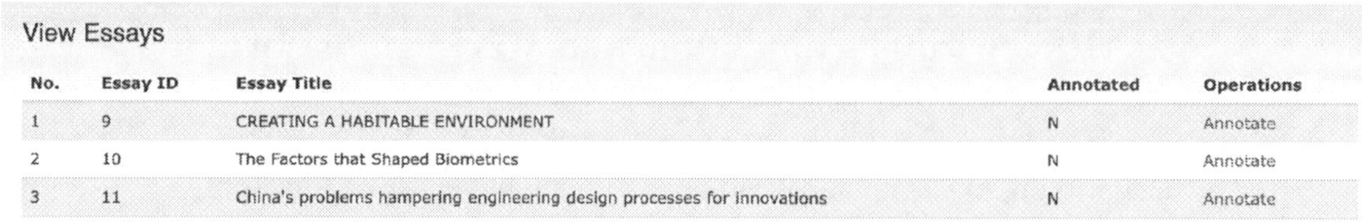
View Essays

No.	Essay ID	Essay Title	Annotated	Operations
1	9	CREATING A HABITABLE ENVIRONMENT	N	Annotate
2	10	The Factors that Shaped Biometrics	N	Annotate
3	11	China's problems hampering engineering design processes for innovations	N	Annotate

Figure 1: The web interface in WAMP for viewing essays.

ing Drupal (version 6.13)[1], a PHP-based content management system. Drupal can be easily customized to extend the functionalities of the software with the use of modules. Other than the community-contributed modules (Appendix A.1) that are shipped together with the Drupal release, a custom module named "WAMP", consisting of two sub-modules "Essay" and "Administration", extends the main functionalities of WAMP.

2.1 WAMP Module

The WAMP module is the parent module that encompasses the two aforementioned sub-modules, and these sub-modules inherit all the functions of the WAMP module. Other than the administrator who manages WAMP, the main user of the software is the "annotator" and the WAMP module specifically contains the navigational user interface for the annotator to view and annotate essays, as illustrated in Figure 1. The WAMP module also allows the administrator to toggle between the mode production or testing (for debugging purpose).

2.2 Essay Sub-Module

The Essay sub-module comprises essay-related management functionalities for the administrator to view all the annotations created by the annotators. Additionally, the administrator can check if an essay has been flagged to be of poor quality or invalid format, and delete the essay to make it unavailable to annotators accordingly. The functionalities for annotating essays are also contained under the Essay sub-module, which will be discussed in more detail under the Annotate Essays subsection.

2.3 Administration Sub-Module

The Administration sub-module is responsible for extending data management functionalities for the administrator, which mainly consists of importing and exporting files. Essays are imported into WAMP in XML (Extensible Markup Language)[2] format. WAMP further processes the imported file to extract the essay title and body, and insert the relevant information into the database. The functionalities for importing essays will be discussed in more detail under the Import Essays subsection. WAMP supports two types of data export: (1) XML and (2) M2. The administrator can export the entire annotation data from the WAMP database into a single XML file. This exported XML file contains the data for all essays and the relevant annotations for all grammatical errors identified and corrected by the annotators. WAMP also allows export of data in M2 file format. Unlike XML export, M2 export is executed for each individual annotator, i.e., the annotation data for a single essay by a single annotator is exported. The exported M2 file contains all the sentences of an essay in separate lines. Each sentence is followed by lines that indicate the start and end word index of the sequence of words identified as an error in the sentence, and the appropriate error type provided by the annotator. Exporting essays will be discussed in greater detail under the Export Essays subsection.

Additionally, under the Administration sub-module, the administrator can also select between two different sets of error tags to be made available to the annotators. Currently, WAMP supports NUCLE (Dahlmeier et al., 2013) as the default set of error tags, with an additional support for the set of ERRANT (Bryant et al., 2017) error tags. NUCLE introduced an extensive list of 28 error tags, ranging from frequently found error types such as verb tense error and subject-verb agreement error, to more niche error types, such as poor citation practice and unclear meaning. Similarly, (Bryant et al., 2017) proposed another error tag scheme that consists of 25 main error types. WAMP is designed in a way that allows easy extension to new sets of error tags. The customization only requires the addition of a new HTML file that contains the

[1] https://www.drupal.org/project/drupal/releases/6.13

[2] https://developer.mozilla.org/en-US/docs/Web/XML/XML_introduction

new error tags and a simple modification to the Administration sub-module. As such, WAMP can be easily customized to accommodate the needs of other GEC research that requires annotated corpora with grammatical errors categorized by a different set of error tags.

3 Functionalities

3.1 Import Essays

Before an annotator can start the annotation on the essays, the administrator first needs to import the essays into WAMP. Each essay has two main components, which are the title and the main body. To import an essay into WAMP, it needs to be in XML format, as illustrated in Figure 2. It is also possible to import multiple essays into WAMP with a single import XML file. Once the XML file is loaded from the database after the upload, the essay is inserted into the database through post-processing of the import XML file. The annotators can now view the list of uploaded essays, as shown in Figure 1, and click on "Annotate" to begin the annotation process.

```
<instance title="CREATING␣A␣HABITABLE␣
    ENVIRONMENT">
    <context>
        Humans have many basic needs and
            one of them is to have an
            environment that can...
        Some countries are having
            difficulties in managing a
            place to live for their
            citizen as they...
    </context>
</instance>
```

Figure 2: An example illustrating the import XML format. The details are explained in Appendix A.2.

3.2 Annotate Essays

Any annotator account can be used to annotate an essay. The following steps to annotate essays are based on the assumptions that (1) an essay has been imported to the database and (2) an annotator account has been created.

An annotator can utilize the WAMP interface to perform annotation on an uploaded essay. However, before the annotator begins to annotate an essay, WAMP allows the annotator to flag the essay to be of poor quality or invalid format. More specifically, if the quality of the essay is very poor and annotations should not be made on it, the annotator can notify the administrator by checking the "Bad Essay" check box. Similarly, if the essay is truncated, poorly formatted, or contains unexpected Unicode characters, the annotator can check the "Needs Editing" check box to notify the administrator to modify the essay before anyone can proceed to annotate the essay. These check boxes can be found in label (4) of Figure 3. The information is shared among all annotators. Hence, if an essay has been flagged as either "Bad Essay" or "Needs Editing", all annotators who have access to the essay will be notified with a warning whenever they load the flagged essay.

3.2.1 Adding Annotations

Once an annotator confirms that there is no issue with an essay, the annotator can proceed with the annotation. The action of annotating an essay can be broken down into three main steps, which are identify, classify, and correct. As shown in label (5) of Figure 3, the annotator can use the cursor to highlight an arbitrary contiguous text span (containing multiple words in general) and identify the grammatical error. Once an error has been highlighted, a pop-up box prompts the annotator to choose the appropriate error type, as illustrated in label (6) of Figure 3. The available error types are based on the predefined set of error tags, configured in the aforementioned Administration sub-module. Lastly, the annotation is completed when the annotator enters an appropriate correction string to correct the error and clicks "Save." Once an annotation is completed, the identified error will be highlighted in yellow with the assigned error tag on top, as indicated in label (7) of Figure 3. Optionally, WAMP allows the annotator to add a comment to clarify the annotation.

3.2.2 Modifying Annotations

WAMP also allows an annotator to modify or delete an existing annotation. After an annotation is saved, clicking on the highlighted text span (as illustrated in label (5) of Figure 3) opens a pop-up window, as shown in Figure 4. The annotator can choose a different error tag, enter another correction string or comment for that annotation by clicking on the "Edit" button. If the annotator considers an existing annotation to be unnecessary, the annotator can simply click on the "Delete" button to delete the annotation from the essay. A sample annotated essay is shown in Figure 5.

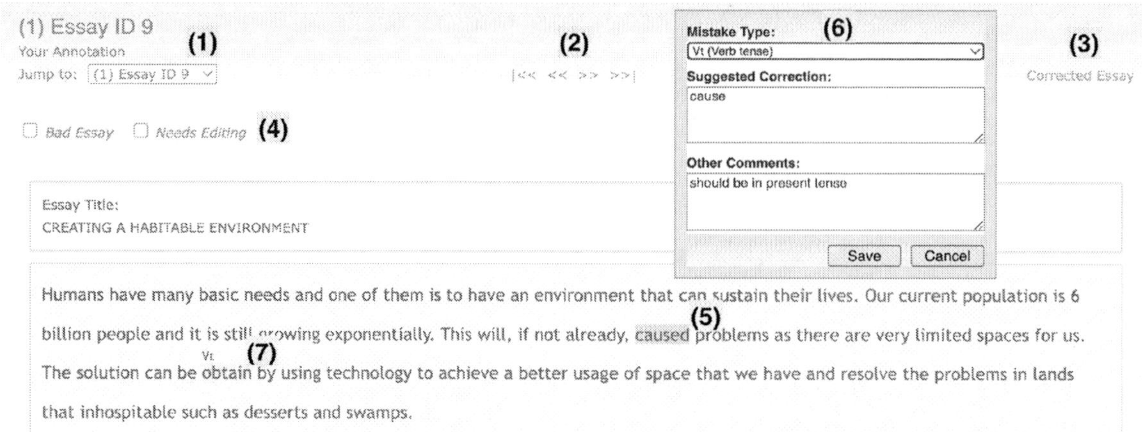

Figure 3: The web interface in WAMP for annotating an essay.

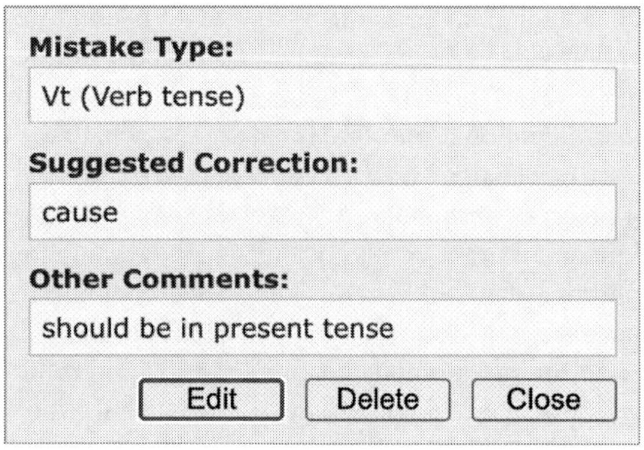

Figure 4: An example illustrating a pop-up menu for annotation.

3.2.3 Characteristics of WAMP

One characteristic of WAMP is that the start (or end) position of an erroneous text span can be the location of any character in an essay, and does not need to be the start (or end) of a word. By allowing annotation in fine granularity and imposing minimal constraints, WAMP provides an environment that closely resembles annotating with pen and paper for the annotators. Additionally, WAMP ensures that no annotation data is lost or damaged during the annotation process by saving changes after every annotation operation. This can prove useful in cases of unexpected connection or hardware failures.

Although WAMP allows multiple annotators to collaborate on annotating the same essay by sharing an annotator account, this workflow is not typical in the context of constructing a GEC corpus. For GEC annotation, it is preferable to have as many different annotations as possible for the same text as there are usually multiple possible ways of correcting an erroneous text (Bryant and Ng, 2015).

Lastly, WAMP allows an annotator to view the corrected version of an annotated essay, which is available as a link in label (3) of Figure 3. The corrected essay simply replaces the existing erroneous text spans with the proposed corrections, displaying each corrected text span in bold and enclosing it within a box. This functionality facilitates the revision of essays for annotators by making it possible to view a corrected essay after the proposed corrections are applied, without having to check each annotation individually. As such, WAMP is unique in that it is an annotation platform that offers an easy interface to highlight errors, classify error types, and view corrected essays.

3.3 Export Essays

Once all the annotation tasks are completed, the administrator can export the annotation data in XML format, as shown in Figure 6. The exported XML file contains all the essays and the annotations that have been saved in the WAMP database so far. WAMP facilitates the export process by allowing extraction of the entire data into a single XML file. The export XML file contains the list of essays that have been uploaded to WAMP. Within each essay are the annotations, if any, and each annotation is identified by the annotator's name to distinguish annotations on the same essay by different annotators.

As previously mentioned, WAMP also supports export of annotation data in M2 format. There are several scorers available to evaluate the performance of GEC systems on a data set and two of the most widely utilized are the MaxMatch

Humans have many basic needs and one of them is to have an environment that can sustain their lives. Our current population is 6 billion people and it is still growing exponentially. This will, if not already, caused (Vt) problems as there are very limited spaces for us. The solution can be obtain (Vform) by using technology to achieve a better usage of space that we have and resolve the problems in lands that inhospitable such as desserts and swamps.

Figure 5: An example illustrating an annotated essay.

```
<annotation annotator="John␣Smith">
    <mistake start="/0.210" end="/0.216"
        >
        <type>Vt</type>
        <correction>cause</correction>
        <comments>should be in present
            tense</comments>
    </mistake>
    <mistake start="/0.287" end="/0.293"
        >
        <type>Vform</type>
        <correction>obtained</correction
            >
        <comments/>
    </mistake>
</annotation>
```

Figure 6: An example illustrating the export XML format. The details are explained in Appendix A.3.

(M^2) scorer (Dahlmeier and Ng, 2012) and the ERRANT (Bryant et al., 2017) scorer. Used as the official GEC scorer for the CoNLL-2013 (Ng et al., 2013) and CoNLL-2014 (Ng et al., 2014) shared tasks, the MaxMatch (M^2) scorer computes the F-score over the optimal phrase-level alignment between a source sentence and a system hypothesis that achieves the highest overlap with the gold-standard annotation (Dahlmeier and Ng, 2012; Náplava et al., 2022). It was also used for other non-English corpora, including the Falko-MERLIN corpus (Boyd, 2018) in German, and the RULEC-GEC corpus (Rozovskaya and Roth, 2019) in Russian. Both the MaxMatch (M^2) scorer and the ERRANT scorer utilize M2 files for evaluation. As shown in Figure 7, the exported M2 file contains a list of tokenized original sentences, preceded by S. Each of these sentences is optionally followed by lines, preceded by A. Each line contains information about an annotation on the associated sentence, including the start and end token offset, the error type, and the tokenized correction string. This indicates that WAMP not only facilitates seamless annotation on essays but also generates annotated gold-standard references that can be further utilized directly for evaluation of GEC system performance.

4 System Implementation

WAMP is a web-based application, built using the LAMP[3] full-stack framework. The specific dependencies are listed in Appendix A.4. To facilitate the deployment of WAMP by standardizing the development environment, we use Docker (version 4.13.1)[4] to set up the required LAMP stack. We build our Docker based on the Docker image[5] of Ubuntu 9.10. After running the Docker image as a standalone container, the source code of WAMP is mounted to the container. One of the benefits of Docker is that other users can easily replicate the environment setup on any device and run the software without having to worry about dependency issues. We believe this is critical for the usability of WAMP and any other annotation tools that serve a similar purpose.

5 Related Work

Grammatical error correction is an active area of research in natural language processing (Chollampatt et al., 2016; Chollampatt and Ng, 2018; Qorib et al., 2022; Bryant et al., 2023). Both commercial (e.g., Grammarly) and open-source GEC tools (e.g., ALLECS (Qorib et al., 2023)) are available. In tandem, the need for new GEC corpora also increases to support GEC development with more training and evaluation data. Unfortunately, as of now, there is no publicly available open-source GEC annotation tool to help with the creation of GEC corpora. Andersen (2011) reported that annotating GEC corpora with a graphical tool can significantly increase the annotation speed compared to using a text editor. The author made a simple annotation tool for the experiment, but the tool is not explained in detail and not publicly available.

One non-free tool that can be used for GEC anno-

[3]https://www.ibm.com/cloud/learn/lamp-stack-explained

[4]https://docs.docker.com/desktop/release-notes/

[5]https://github.com/iComputer7/ancient-ubuntu-docker

```
S This will , if not already , caused problems as there are very limited spaces for us .
A 7 8|||Vt|||cause|||REQUIRED|||-NONE-|||0

S The solution can be obtain by using technology to achieve a better usage of space that we
have and resolve the problems in lands that inhospitable such as desserts and swamps .
A 4 5|||Vform|||obtained|||REQUIRED|||-NONE-|||0
```

Figure 7: An example illustrating the exported M2 format.

tation is Write&Improve[6], which is an online platform to assist English learners to improve their writing (Yannakoudakis et al., 2018). Write&Improve allows English learners to submit their essays and get feedback from an automated system or a teacher. In our experience of using Write&Improve, we could not find a way of labeling error type when annotating a text. Furthermore, the system is unable to export the list of corrections to be applied to a text, which is important for the GEC task. This is because the system was designed to focus more on tracking students' learning progress instead of creating a GEC corpus. The lack of error-type labeling and correction export features is also the reason why text rewriting tools (Xu et al., 2019; Goldfarb-Tarrant et al., 2019) are not suitable for GEC annotation.

Kutuzov and Kuzmenko (2015) designed a tool for grammatical error detection (GED) annotation by integrating BRAT (Stenetorp et al., 2012) with a linguistic analyzer (FreeLing (Padró and Stanilovsky, 2012)) and a spellchecker (Aspell[7]). BRAT is a multi-task text annotation tool that can be used for part-of-speech tagging, named entity recognition, dependency parsing, and other NLP tasks. BRAT has an intuitive interface similar to WAMP, but BRAT is not suitable for GEC corpora annotation. This is because for each text span, one can only assign a label from a pre-determined list of labels instead of providing a free-form correction string. This is also the reason why other sequence-tagging annotation tools (Yang et al., 2018; Zhang et al., 2021) are not suitable for GEC annotation, which requires associating a text span with a free-form correction string and a label for its error type.

Machine translation post-editing tools (Lee et al., 2021) or text simplification annotation tools (Stodden and Kallmeyer, 2022) are also not suitable for GEC annotation, because the tools expect a pair of sentences for each data instance. This means that the annotator needs to rewrite the whole text in full first, then aligns the words in both sentences. This will result in excessive rewriting and a slower annotation process, compared to manual annotation with a text editor.

In summary, GEC annotation needs a specialized tool that cannot be easily substituted by other natural language processing annotation tools.

6 Conclusion

In this paper, we introduce WAMP, a web-based annotation platform to facilitate the process of manual annotation and export the annotation data in XML and M2 format. WAMP has already proven its utility in building the NUCLE corpus, a large annotated corpus that contains over one million words which are completely annotated by professional English instructors using WAMP (Dahlmeier et al., 2013). With the new enhancements in place, WAMP brings even greater values in generating annotations for annotated corpora by offering more flexibility in defining the error tags and converting the annotation data into the M2 file format that can be used as references for evaluating GEC systems.

For future work, WAMP can be extended to include learning analytics features, such as keeping track of the counts of different error types made by different groups of learners. This will facilitate the analysis of the error profile of different learners and enable personalized and targeted assistance to learners.

Acknowledgements

We thank Jun Hong Pua and Hong Guan Chan for implementing WAMP. This research is supported by the National Research Foundation, Singapore under its AI Singapore Programme (AISG Award No: AISG-RP-2019-014).

Limitations

As an annotation tool, WAMP is tailored for the text correction task, by allowing a user to easily highlight any span of text and adding the corrected text as replacement. As such, WAMP is less suitable as an annotation tool for other natural language

[6] https://writeandimprove.com/
[7] http://aspell.net/

processing tasks such as named entity recognition, coreference resolution, etc.

References

Øistein E. Andersen. 2011. Semi-automatic ESOL error annotation. *English Profile Journal*, 2:e1.

Adriane Boyd. 2018. Using Wikipedia edits in low resource grammatical error correction. In *Proceedings of the 2018 EMNLP Workshop W-NUT: The 4th Workshop on Noisy User-generated Text*, pages 79–84, Brussels, Belgium. Association for Computational Linguistics.

Christopher Bryant, Mariano Felice, and Ted Briscoe. 2017. Automatic annotation and evaluation of error types for grammatical error correction. In *Proceedings of the 55th Annual Meeting of the Association for Computational Linguistics (Volume 1: Long Papers)*, pages 793–805, Vancouver, Canada. Association for Computational Linguistics.

Christopher Bryant and Hwee Tou Ng. 2015. How far are we from fully automatic high quality grammatical error correction? In *Proceedings of the 53rd Annual Meeting of the Association for Computational Linguistics and the 7th International Joint Conference on Natural Language Processing (Volume 1: Long Papers)*, pages 697–707, Beijing, China. Association for Computational Linguistics.

Christopher Bryant, Zheng Yuan, Muhammad Reza Qorib, Hannan Cao, Hwee Tou Ng, and Ted Briscoe. 2023. Grammatical error correction: A survey of the state of the art. *Computational Linguistics*, 49(3).

Shamil Chollampatt and Hwee Tou Ng. 2018. A multilayer convolutional encoder-decoder neural network for grammatical error correction. In *Proceedings of the Thirty-Second AAAI Conference on Artificial Intelligence*, pages 5755–5762.

Shamil Chollampatt, Kaveh Taghipour, and Hwee Tou Ng. 2016. Neural network translation models for grammatical error correction. In *Proceedings of the Twenty-Fifth International Joint Conference on Artificial Intelligence*, pages 2768–2774.

Daniel Dahlmeier and Hwee Tou Ng. 2012. Better evaluation for grammatical error correction. In *Proceedings of the 2012 Conference of the North American Chapter of the Association for Computational Linguistics: Human Language Technologies*, pages 568–572, Montréal, Canada. Association for Computational Linguistics.

Daniel Dahlmeier, Hwee Tou Ng, and Siew Mei Wu. 2013. Building a large annotated corpus of learner English: The NUS corpus of learner English. In *Proceedings of the Eighth Workshop on Innovative Use of NLP for Building Educational Applications*, pages 22–31, Atlanta, Georgia. Association for Computational Linguistics.

Seraphina Goldfarb-Tarrant, Haining Feng, and Nanyun Peng. 2019. Plan, write, and revise: an interactive system for open-domain story generation. In *Proceedings of the 2019 Conference of the North American Chapter of the Association for Computational Linguistics (Demonstrations)*, pages 89–97, Minneapolis, Minnesota. Association for Computational Linguistics.

Andrey Kutuzov and Elizaveta Kuzmenko. 2015. Semi-automated typical error annotation for learner English essays: integrating frameworks. In *Proceedings of the fourth workshop on NLP for computer-assisted language learning*, pages 35–41, Vilnius, Lithuania. LiU Electronic Press.

Dongjun Lee, Junhyeong Ahn, Heesoo Park, and Jaemin Jo. 2021. IntelliCAT: Intelligent machine translation post-editing with quality estimation and translation suggestion. In *Proceedings of the 59th Annual Meeting of the Association for Computational Linguistics and the 11th International Joint Conference on Natural Language Processing: System Demonstrations*, pages 11–19, Online. Association for Computational Linguistics.

Jakub Náplava, Milan Straka, Jana Straková, and Alexandr Rosen. 2022. Czech grammar error correction with a large and diverse corpus. *Transactions of the Association for Computational Linguistics*, 10:452–467.

Mariana Neves and Jurica Ševa. 2019. An extensive review of tools for manual annotation of documents. *Briefings in Bioinformatics*, 22(1):146–163.

Hwee Tou Ng, Siew Mei Wu, Ted Briscoe, Christian Hadiwinoto, Raymond Hendy Susanto, and Christopher Bryant. 2014. The CoNLL-2014 shared task on grammatical error correction. In *Proceedings of the Eighteenth Conference on Computational Natural Language Learning: Shared Task*, pages 1–14, Baltimore, Maryland. Association for Computational Linguistics.

Hwee Tou Ng, Siew Mei Wu, Yuanbin Wu, Christian Hadiwinoto, and Joel Tetreault. 2013. The CoNLL-2013 shared task on grammatical error correction. In *Proceedings of the Seventeenth Conference on Computational Natural Language Learning: Shared Task*, pages 1–12, Sofia, Bulgaria. Association for Computational Linguistics.

Lluís Padró and Evgeny Stanilovsky. 2012. FreeLing 3.0: Towards wider multilinguality. In *Proceedings of the Eighth International Conference on Language Resources and Evaluation (LREC'12)*, pages 2473–2479, Istanbul, Turkey. European Language Resources Association (ELRA).

Muhammad Qorib, Seung-Hoon Na, and Hwee Tou Ng. 2022. Frustratingly easy system combination for grammatical error correction. In *Proceedings of the 2022 Conference of the North American Chapter of the Association for Computational Linguistics:*

Human Language Technologies, pages 1964–1974, Seattle, United States. Association for Computational Linguistics.

Muhammad Reza Qorib, Geonsik Moon, and Hwee Tou Ng. 2023. ALLECS: A lightweight language error correction system. In *Proceedings of the 17th Conference of the European Chapter of the Association for Computational Linguistics: System Demonstrations*, pages 298–306, Dubrovnik, Croatia. Association for Computational Linguistics.

Alla Rozovskaya and Dan Roth. 2019. Grammar error correction in morphologically rich languages: The case of Russian. *Transactions of the Association for Computational Linguistics*, 7:1–17.

Charanjit Swaran Singh, Amreet Jageer Singh, Nur Qistina Abdul Razak, and Thilaga Ravinthar. 2017. Grammar errors made by ESL tertiary students in writing. *English Language Teaching*, 10:16.

Pontus Stenetorp, Sampo Pyysalo, Goran Topić, Tomoko Ohta, Sophia Ananiadou, and Jun'ichi Tsujii. 2012. brat: a web-based tool for NLP-assisted text annotation. In *Proceedings of the Demonstrations at the 13th Conference of the European Chapter of the Association for Computational Linguistics*, pages 102–107, Avignon, France. Association for Computational Linguistics.

Regina Stodden and Laura Kallmeyer. 2022. TS-ANNO: An annotation tool to build, annotate and evaluate text simplification corpora. In *Proceedings of the 60th Annual Meeting of the Association for Computational Linguistics: System Demonstrations*, pages 145–155, Dublin, Ireland. Association for Computational Linguistics.

Qiongkai Xu, Chenchen Xu, and Lizhen Qu. 2019. ALTER: Auxiliary text rewriting tool for natural language generation. In *Proceedings of the 2019 Conference on Empirical Methods in Natural Language Processing and the 9th International Joint Conference on Natural Language Processing (EMNLP-IJCNLP): System Demonstrations*, pages 13–18, Hong Kong, China. Association for Computational Linguistics.

Jie Yang, Yue Zhang, Linwei Li, and Xingxuan Li. 2018. YEDDA: A lightweight collaborative text span annotation tool. In *Proceedings of ACL 2018, System Demonstrations*, pages 31–36, Melbourne, Australia. Association for Computational Linguistics.

Helen Yannakoudakis, Øistein E. Andersen, Ardeshir Geranpayeh, Ted Briscoe, and Diane Nicholls. 2018. Developing an automated writing placement system for esl learners. *Applied Measurement in Education*, 31:251–267.

Baoli Zhang, Zhucong Li, Zhen Gan, Yubo Chen, Jing Wan, Kang Liu, Jun Zhao, Shengping Liu, and Yafei Shi. 2021. CroAno : A crowd annotation platform for improving label consistency of Chinese NER dataset. In *Proceedings of the 2021 Conference on Empirical Methods in Natural Language Processing: System Demonstrations*, pages 275–282, Online and Punta Cana, Dominican Republic. Association for Computational Linguistics.

A Appendix

A.1 WAMP Modules

WAMP contains the following community-contributed modules:

- Conditional Styles (version 6.x-1.1)
- Hovertip (version 6.x-1.x-dev)
- Jquery Update (version 6.x-2.x).

A.2 Import XML

The import XML file encompasses a list of "instance" elements, as shown in Figure 2. Each "instance" element represents an individual essay to be imported into WAMP and is characterized by a "title" attribute that serves as the title of the specified essay. Under the "instance" element is the "context" element that contains the actual content of the essay. Inside the "context" element, each paragraph is separated by double line breaks and can contain multiple sentences.

A.3 Export XML

The export XML format contains a list of "instance" elements, which represent individual essays imported into WAMP. Each of these "instance" elements, characterized by the "title" attribute, has two main types of child elements, "context" and "annotation." The "context" element comprises the main body of the essay and the "annotation" element contains the annotation XML format. The annotation XML format, shown in Figure 6, is specific to a single essay and by a single annotator. The root element of the annotation XML format is "annotation", which contains a child element "mistake" representing a single annotation. The "start" and "end" attributes denote the start and end position of the specified grammatical error that is annotated. For example, the annotation for "cause," illustrated in Figure 3, is represented as having start attribute of "/0.210" and end attribute of "/0.216." This indicates that the annotation belongs to the 0th line (counting from 0) and the annotation spans from the 210th to 216th character offset positions within that line. Also, the "mistake" element includes three sub-child elements, "type", "correction", and "comments." Each of these sub-child elements contains information about the error type, proposed correction, and comment respectively.

A.4 Docker Dependencies

- Ubuntu (version 9.10)[8]
- Apache (version 2.2)[9]
- PHP (version 5.2)[10]
- MySQL (version 5.1)[11]

[8]https://old-releases.ubuntu.com/releases/karmic/

[9]https://httpd.apache.org/download.cgi

[10]https://www.php.net/releases/index.php

[11]https://downloads.mysql.com/archives/community/

Association for Computational Linguistics
209 N. Eighth Street
Stroudsburg, Pennsylvania 18360

ISBN 978-1-7138-9001-0

CURRAN ASSOCIATES INC.
proceedings.com